S·H·P
THE
SCHOOLS
HISTORY
PROJECT

DISCOVERING THE PAST

BRITAIN &
THE GREAT WAR

Greg Hetherton
Series Editor: Colin Shephard (Director, SHP)

JOHN MURRAY

Acknowledgements

Illustrations by: David Anstey; Art Construction; Peter Bull Art Studio; Steve Smith.

Illustration on p.25 reproduced by kind permission of Fleetway Editions Ltd.

Photographs reproduced by kind permission of:
cover Imperial War Museum, London. **p.4** The Illustrated London News Picture Library. **p.5** *both* The Hulton Deutsch Collection. **p.6** *top* Michael Holford; *bottom* Greater London Photograph Library. **p.7** *top left* Topham; *top right* The Illustrated London News Picture Library; *centre left and right* Mary Evans Picture Library; *bottom* Reproduced by permission of *Punch*. **p.8** *top centre* and *centre* The Hulton Deutsch Collection; *bottom left* Topham; *bottom right* Beamish, The North of England Open Air Museum, Co. Durham. **p.9** *both* The Hulton Deutsch Collection. **p.10** *all* Mary Evans Picture Library. **p.11** *top* Mary Evans Picture Library; *bottom* The Hulton Deutsch Collection. **p.20** *all* Imperial War Museum, London. **p.21** *centre left* Imperial War Museum, London; *bottom* The Illustrated London News Picture Library. **p.22** Peter Newark's Historical Pictures. **p.23** *both*, **pp.26-27** *all*, **p.29** *top* Imperial War Museum, London. **p.30** *top* National Museum of Labour History. **p.30** *centre* and *bottom*, **p.34** *all*, **p.35** *bottom* Imperial War Museum, London. **p.35** *top* Tate Gallery, London. **p.38** Imperial War Museum, London. **p.39** Copyright © BBC. **p.41** Imperial War Museum, London. **p.42** Reproduced by permission of *Punch*. **pp.44-46** *all* Imperial War Museum, London. **p.47** The Tank Museum. **pp.48-49** *all* Imperial War Museum, London. **p.50** *both* Peter Newark's Historical Pictures. **p.51** *both*, **p.53** *top* Imperial War Museum, London. **p.53** *bottom* Popperfoto. **pp.54-55** *all*, **p.57** *bottom* Imperial War Museum, London. **p.59** Fitzwilliam Museum, University of Cambridge. **p.61** *top* National Museum of Labour History; *bottom* Imperial War Museum, London. **p.62** The Hulton Deutsch Collection. **p.63** *top right* John Johnson Collection, Bodleian Library; *rest* Mary Evans Picture Library. **p.64** Mansell Collection. **p.65** Mary Evans Picture Library. **p.67** Southampton City Heritage (Oral Heritage). **p.69** *top* Warwickshire County Museum; *bottom* Mary Evans Picture Library.

Pupils' Book ISBN 0–7195–5148–X
Teachers' Evaluation Pack ISBN 0–7195–5152–8

© Greg Hetherton, 1993

First published in 1993
by John Murray (Publishers) Ltd
50 Albemarle Street, London W1X 4BD

Reprinted 1993, 1994

Printed in Hong Kong by Shek Wah Tong Printing Press Ltd.

A CIP catalogue record for this book is available from the British Library
ISBN 0–7195–5148–X

Note: The wording and sentence structure of some written sources have been adapted and simplified to make them accessible to all pupils, while faithfully preserving the sense of the original. A bibliography is provided in the Teachers' Resource Book.

The extract from *Blackadder Goes Forth* on p.39 is reproduced by kind permission of Richard Curtis and Ben Elton.

Vera Brittain's poem *To My Brother* from *Testament of Youth* is included with the permission of Paul Berry, her Literary Executor, and Victor Gollancz Ltd.

Extracts from Richard Aldington's poem *Trench Idyll* are reproduced by permission of Rosica Colin Limited. © The Estate of Richard Aldington

Poems and prose by Siegfried Sassoon are reproduced by permission of George Sassoon.

Every effort has been made to trace all the copyright holders, but if any have been inadvertently overlooked the publishers will be pleased to make the necessary arrangement at the first opportunity.

THE SCHOOLS HISTORY PROJECT

This project was set up by the Schools Council in 1972. Its main aim was to suggest suitable objectives for History teachers, and to promote the use of appropriate materials and teaching methods for their realisation. This involved a reconsideration of the nature of History and its relevance in secondary schools, the design of a syllabus framework which shows the uses of History in the education of adolescents, and the setting up of appropriate examinations.

Since 1978 the project has been based at Trinity and All Saints' College, Leeds, where it is one of three curriculum development projects run and supported by the Centre for History Education. The project is now self funding and with the advent of the National Curriculum it has expanded its publications to provide courses throughout the Key Stages for pupils aged 5–16. The project provides INSET for all aspects of National Curriculum History.

Contents

N.B. Words in SMALL CAPITALS are defined in the glossary on page 72.

Edwardian Britain: the Golden Age?

IN 1901 Queen Victoria died. The period between her death and the outbreak of the Great War in 1914 is known as the Edwardian period. It was seen by many people at the time, and by historians since, as a 'golden age'. It was as if the sun always shone and everyone was having a good time. It was the perfect time to be alive. Some historians believe that all this was destroyed for ever by the Great War, or the First World War as it is now called.

This book will help you to decide:
- whether the time before the Great War was a golden age for everybody
- whether the War destroyed this golden age and made everyone's lives worse
- whether things would have changed anyway even without the War.

The Edwardian period

Edward VII became king in 1901. He was nearly 60 years old, and had waited a long time to become king. During that time he lived a very different life from that of his mother, Queen Victoria. He loved having a good time. He gambled and hunted and loved horse racing: his horses won the Derby three times and the Grand National once. He surrounded himself with the most beautiful women of the time, and had affairs with several actresses.

SOURCE 1 The future King Edward VII leading his horse into the winner's enclosure at the 1896 Derby

Between 1903 and 1913 the amount ► spent by local councils on children's education increased from £10 million to over £30 million

◄ **1906** Workman's Compensation Act. A worker who was injured by an accident at work or caught a disease at work could claim compensation

1908 Old Age Pensions introduced: ► five shillings a week for people over 70 with an income of less that £21 a year

When he finally became king, it was clear that the serious days of Queen Victoria were over. When he was crowned in 1902 he held massive banquets for the poor, which cost over £30,000 – an enormous sum of money in those days. He was a very popular king, and had a big influence on the way many other people led their lives.

For the rich – the upper class and the middle class – it was a time of great comfort and luxury. They lived in comfortable houses with large gardens. Many of them had so much money they did not need to work. But they had a busy time watching polo at Ranelagh, horse racing at Ascot or yachting at Cowes, going to dinner parties or dances, or watching the opera.

Edward made popular the idea that the weekend was a time for rest and leisure. Many people used the weekends for going to the seaside.

At home the upper and middle classes had servants to do most of their housework and cooking. A whole class of British society grew up never needing to do anything around the house, however simple. These people never had to make a pot of tea, wash up, mend or iron clothes, post a letter, or even brush their own hair or choose their own clothes.

At this time fashions were changing. Houses became lighter than Victorian homes and less cluttered with heavy furniture. White paint and light-coloured wallpaper replaced heavy reds and browns. Glass conservatories became popular.

1911 National Insurance Act. Workers and employers made weekly contributions which were used to give workers sickness benefit and free medical care. In trades like building, where there was a lot of temporary unemployment, unemployment pay was also given

SOURCE 2 Reforms introduced during the Edwardian period

Women's clothing fashions changed as well. They wore dresses that gave them a tiny waist and a full bosom. Some skirts were made so tight round the ankles that only small steps were possible.

Motor cars were beginning to be a common sight on the roads. In London horse-drawn buses were being replaced by petrol-driven buses and trams.

The rich believed in progress. They were sure that their lives were better than their parents' and that things would go on getting better all the time!

Now let's see if the poor had any reason to believe that things were getting better.

Between 1901 and 1914 the measures shown in Source 2 began to give the poor some protection against the worst evils of the Victorian period.

SOURCE 3 A photograph taken in 1912. The family lived in this one room

SOURCE 4 The living room of a skilled worker's house, 1910. This man worked in the engineering industry. There were five rooms in his house

SOURCE 5 Houses in Hampstead Garden Suburb on the outskirts of London. They were built in 1905 to provide cheap housing for all classes of people

SOURCE 6 Providence Place, Stepney, East London, in 1909

SOURCE 7 From an article written in 1913

> Mr H. is 22 and works in a brewery. He earns £1 per week. He gives his wife, who is twenty, all of his wage. They have one child of six months.
>
> His wife used to work in a polish factory, but she was dismissed (and paid a small bonus) when she got married, because the firm does not employ married women. She is an excellent housewife and keeps their one room clean and comfortable . . .

SOURCE 8 From a biography of Daisy and Walter Thackrah, written by their son. They rented a house in Hampstead Garden Suburb (see Source 5)

> Spring 1914 was a beautiful time for them both. Things grew and budded in the garden . . . They walked through the two woods in the road and across the fields all around them . . .
>
> Daisy sang at her housework, which was soon done in the morning. She needed only to go to the shops once or twice a week. She was a little bored in the afternoons except for the tea parties with the neighbours, and she looked forward impatiently to Walter's return, which was so often late in the evening. It would be all right when she had a family . . .

SOURCE 9 A middle-class woman describes moving into her new house in 1900

> We modernised it with a service lift [to bring food and water upstairs from the kitchen in the basement], electric light and a telephone.
>
> The house contained a large basement, three sitting rooms, a lounge–hall and seven bedrooms. All the rooms were warmed by coal fires, there were nursery meals to be carried up and down, hot water to be taken to the bedrooms, and we entertained a great deal. Yet we found little difficulty of running the house with a staff of a nurse, a parlour maid, a housemaid and a cook. Later we kept a manservant for £70 a year. The cook earned £28. The nurse's salary was £40.

SOURCE 10 From a survey by Seebohm Rowntree in York in 1901. He calculated that a family of two adults and three children could just live on 21s 8d a week. Nearly half the workers in the country earned less than 20s a week

> [To manage on 21s 8d] . . . they must never spend a penny on a railway or bus fare. They must never purchase a half penny newspaper. The children must have no pocket money for dolls, marbles or sweets. The father must smoke no tobacco, and must drink no beer. The mother must never buy pretty clothes for herself or for her children. Finally, the wage-earner must never be absent from his work for a single day.

SOURCE 11 Children at the seaside in 1909

SOURCE 14 People drinking tea outside the clubhouse at Ranelagh, painted in 1907

SOURCE 12
Ladies' fashions
in 1914

SOURCE 13 'A Quiet Sunday in Our Village' from *Punch*, 6 June 1906

1. Which of Sources 1–14 show or describe
   ■ poor working-class families who lived hard lives
   ■ very rich families who lived comfortable lives?
   Give reasons for all your choices.
2. Are there any sources you have not included in your answer to question 1? What type of people do these show?
3. What hardships did poor working-class families have to face in their daily lives? Support your answers with evidence from the sources.
4. Make a list of the differences you can find between the lives of the rich and the lives of the poor.
5. What does the role of women seem to be?
6. From the evidence in these sources write an essay entitled 'Was the period 1901–1914 a golden age?'

Was the Golden Age coming to an end?

FOR 150 years Britain's trade and industry had been growing quickly. Middle-class owners and managers had made a lot of money out of industry. Some skilled workers had also done well – their wages were good, they could afford small but respectable houses, and they were proud of their position in society.

However, in the large industrial towns, such as London, Leeds and Manchester, many men, women and children as young as ten worked as unskilled labourers in factories. The conditions were often dangerous. The wages were low and the hours were long. The same problems were faced by miners and by labourers in the countryside.

Work was divided into 'women's jobs' and 'men's jobs'. It was assumed that women could only do light, indoor work which did not need strength or skill. Women were usually paid less than men, even though they worked the same hours. Thirteen million men had paid jobs, but only five and a half million women. Many married women worked at home, either as housewives or making clothes or doing laundry for desperately low wages in the room where they lived, ate and slept.

An alternative to this for a young, unmarried girl was to work as a domestic servant. In domestic work pay was low, a fifteen- to sixteen-hour day was quite normal and there was hardly any free time, even at weekends.

Source 1 shows you the kind of work women were doing outside their homes in 1914.

1. Can you think of any jobs today that are usually regarded as 'men's' or 'women's' jobs? Why is this?

Percentage of workforce

Domestic service
Textiles/clothing
Food/drink/tobacco
Transport
Manufacturing/engineering
Farming/forestry
Mining/quarrying/building

Total workforce

Key
Women Men

▲SOURCE 1 Percentages of men and women workers in various industries in 1914

▼SOURCE 2 A hat factory in Manchester, 1909

▲SOURCE 4 Women telephone switchboard operators

SOURCE 3 Women haymaking

SOURCE 5 A reconstruction of a Co-op shop in 1913

2. From the evidence on page 8 make a list of jobs that were done mainly by women, jobs done mainly by men and jobs done by either.

3. Women were not allowed to work down mines, but young boys were. What does this tell you about attitudes at this time?

Protests on the eve of war

Even before the Great War broke out in 1914, there were signs that the Golden Age was coming to an end.

In the years before the War, the poor became even worse off. More people were unemployed. Those who had jobs found that although prices were going up their wages were not. The dockers were still being paid the 'dockers' tanner' (6d an hour) they had fought for in 1889! More and more workers joined trade unions to get their pay and working conditions improved.

The poor found their living conditions hard to bear because they could see that the rich were still living a life of luxury. Some union leaders called for all the unions to join together in a massive strike. This would bring both industry and the government to their knees and the unions could then take over the running of the country. Many workers did not want to go as far as this, but from 1910 until 1914 strikes broke out in all parts of the country. Many of them were very violent.

SOURCE 7 A photograph taken in 1912, when London was running out of food due to a transport strike. Police are escorting this meat van into London

The leading strikers were the railwaymen, the dockers and the miners. The government called in new workers to replace the strikers and used troops to protect these workers. The troops even did some jobs, such as running the trains.

In 1911 one million workers went on strike. In 1913 the three big unions, the railwaymen, the transport workers and the miners, formed an alliance to organise a general strike of all workers. Some historians believe the government would have been defeated by these powerful unions if the War had not broken out.

SOURCE 8 From a book by G. Dangerfield called *The Strange Death of Liberal England*, written in 1937. Here he is describing the effects of the dockers' strike in 1912

66 *Everything began to die – coal and water services, gas and electricity, railway, road and river transport. As for the butter trade, the Danish butter came in casks and was not refrigerated; it was growing rancid in the mounting heat. The frozen meat from Argentina and New Zealand – on which London depended – was going bad. Famine drew nearer by the hour.* 99

SOURCE 6 London policemen marching into Tonypandy in South Wales in 1910. They later clashed with striking miners

Another group posed a threat to law and order during this period: women. You might expect that poor women suffering from appalling living and working conditions would cause trouble for the government, but in fact the leaders of the protesters were often rich, well educated women. They were protesting because they wanted the right to vote in elections.

Many women believed that unless they were given the right to vote they would not be able to improve their living and working conditions. The Women's Social and Political Union (WSPU) was formed in 1903 to try and persuade the government to give women the vote (suffrage). It was led by Mrs Emmeline Pankhurst, and its members were known as the Suffragettes.

> **SOURCE 9** A speech by Mrs Pankhurst in 1913
>
> *It was rapidly becoming clear to my mind that men regarded women as a servant class in the community and that women were going to remain in that class until they lifted themselves out of it. I asked myself many times, what was to be done?*

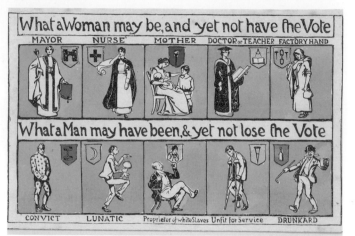

SOURCE 11 A Suffragette postcard of 1910

1. Look back at page 9. What aims did the strikers and the Suffragettes have in common?
2. How did their aims differ?
3. Can you think of any argument that a man might have used to disagree with the comments in Source 11?

It may seem difficult for us today to understand why women were not allowed to vote, but at that time many men thought women could not make sensible decisions, and that politics was a man's business. Even those who supported women's right to vote were worried that, because women outnumbered men, women would have too much influence.

In 1910 the House of Commons voted on whether women should be given the vote. A Bill was actually passed by a large majority of 139. But in November Parliament was dissolved before the measure became law. Women tried to meet the Prime Minister to get him to promise to keep the Bill, but he refused. A violent protest followed – 119 women were arrested and two died from injuries received in the skirmishes.

From 1910 onwards the protests of the women campaigners became increasingly violent. Two distinct groups of women campaigners emerged, the Suffragettes and the Suffragists. The Suffragists were moderates. They held meetings and demonstrations and tried to persuade politicians by argument that women should have the vote.

The Suffragettes became more extreme. They were prepared to break the law in order to get what they wanted. They chained themselves to the railings of MPs' houses, set fire to pillar boxes, attacked policemen, broke shop windows and slashed pictures

SOURCE 10 Two postcards produced by the Suffragettes

in the National Gallery. They attacked property, such as 'men only' golf courses. One died when she threw herself at the King's horse during the Derby of 1913.

4. Sources 12–14 illustrate various actions by women campaigners. Which would be approved by the Suffragists? Which by the Suffragettes?

SOURCE 14
A Suffragette poster showing a prisoner being force fed

SOURCE 12 From the *Daily Telegraph* newspaper, 2 March 1912

❝ *A band of women set out on such a window breaking campaign in the main streets of the West End as London has ever known. For a quarter of an hour, nothing was to be heard in the Strand, Downing Street, Piccadilly and Oxford Street but falling, shattered glass. Women who a moment before had appeared to be on peaceful shopping expeditions, produced from their bags hammers, stones and sticks and began an attack on the nearest windows.* ❞

SOURCE 13 A peaceful demonstration in 1912

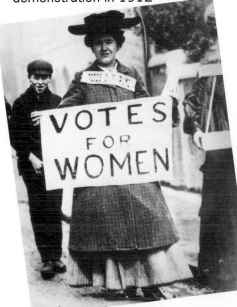

Between 1912 and 1914 the pressure mounted. The Suffragettes' campaign became more and more violent. They bombed the Chancellor of the Exchequer Lloyd George's newly built house, and set fire to public buildings and property.

The government was determined not to give in to violence. Many Suffragettes were put in prison. Some went on hunger strike. If Suffragettes died in prison they might gain public support, so the government force fed them. In turn, the Suffragettes produced posters such as Source 14 which made this government policy unpopular. So in 1913 the government passed the so-called 'Cat and Mouse Act'. This let women out of prison if their health became bad, but they were arrested again when they had recovered.

In 1910 it had seemed as if women would soon get the vote. But by 1914 it seemed the movement was getting nowhere. The Suffragettes were losing public support because of their violent protests. The government was as determined as ever not to give in to them. Their right to vote seemed as far away as ever.

5. Why do you think the government introduced the 'Cat and Mouse Act'?
6. Using the information on pages 10–11 say whether you think the Suffragettes' campaign had been successful up to 1914.
7. Who were the greater threat to the government, the strikers or the Suffragettes?

1. Put this heading in your book: '1914: Are the good times coming to an end for Britain?'
Divide your page in half. Head one column 'yes' and write in it evidence that suggests they were. Head the other column 'no' and write in it evidence to suggest they were not.
Then come to a conclusion, explaining your answer.

Why did war break out in 1914?

Was war expected in Europe?

Source 1 shows Europe in 1914. For a number of years tension between the main European powers had been increasing. Each country had been openly building up its military strength.

In 1914 there were two main power blocks:
- **the Triple Entente:** Great Britain, France and Russia (formed in 1907)
- **the Triple Alliance:** Germany, Italy and Austria–Hungary (formed in 1882).

Each member of the alliances promised to help its allies if they were attacked by a country belonging to the other alliance.

SOURCE 1 Europe in 1914

1. Draw a grid with six columns, one each for Britain, France, Russia, Germany, Austria–Hungary and Italy. Using the information in Source 1, fill in population, number of soldiers, number of warships, overseas empire (tick or cross) and main rivals and friends for each one.
2. Which of the six countries do you think was the strongest in 1914? Give your reasons.
3. Which alliance do you think was stronger?
4. Is there any reason why Germany might want to attack Britain?
5. Do you think that if war broke out between two of these countries, all the other countries would be dragged in as well? Explain your answer.

Britain
Britain had a large empire and a strong navy; it had been the main industrial country in Europe for over 100 years.
- Main concern: Germany's growing strength. For example, Germany was now producing more iron and steel than Britain; Germany was building a navy as big as Britain's; Germany was expanding its empire

GREAT BRITAIN
45 million
711,000
185
64
£ 50 million
Empire 390 million

BELGIUM

FRANCE

Germany
Germany had only become a united country in 1871, but by 1914 it had built up a strong army and navy and the start of an overseas empire. The Kaiser wanted Germany to become a 'world-wide power'.
- Main concerns: Jealousy of Britain's Empire and wealth; fear of having unfriendly countries (France and Russia) on its eastern and western borders

65 million
2,200,000
97
23
£ 60 million
Empire 15 million

RUSSIA

Alsace–Lorraine   GERMANY

SWITZERLAND

AUSTRIA–HUNGARY

40 million
1,250,000
62
73
£ 37 million
Empire 58 million

ITALY

Bosnia

France
Until 1870, France had been one of the most powerful countries in Europe. Like Britain, it had a large empire.
- Main concern: Revenge! In 1871 France had lost two of its regions – Alsace and Lorraine – to the Germans as a result of a war. It wanted them back

Italy
Italy was on the side of Germany and Austria–Hungary. However, it hoped to gain land from Austria–Hungary as its Empire collapsed.
- Main concern: to remain neutral in the event of war

35 million
750,000
36
12
£ 10 million
Empire 2,000,000

SPAIN

Was war expected in Britain?

Under the Triple Entente Britain promised to help France if it was attacked by Germany. Anti-German feeling had been building up in Britain long before 1914. People in many walks of life openly discussed the German threat. By 1914 a German attack on France seemed very likely. People expected that such an attack could trigger off a war in Europe. Sources 2–4 are extracts from the many novels, articles, letters and speeches which dealt with this subject.

SOURCE 2 From the *Daily Mail* newspaper, 1909

> *Germany is deliberately preparing to destroy the British Empire . . . We are all to be drilled and schooled and uniformed by German officials. Britain alone stands in the way of Germany's path to world power and domination.*

SOURCE 3 From *Howards End*, a novel by E.M. Forster, written in 1910

> *The remark 'England and Germany are bound to fight' makes war a little more likely each time that it is made, and is therefore made more often by the gutter press of each nation.*

SOURCE 4 From a letter written by David Lloyd George to Winston Churchill in 1911. They were both powerful politicians and future prime ministers

> *I have been reading the Foreign Office papers. They are full of menace. The thunderclouds are gathering. I am not at all sure that we are prepared or are preparing . . . I am inclined to think that the chances of war are increasing.*

1. Source 3 is from a novel. Can it help us to understand whether people in Britain expected war? Explain your answer.
2. Which sources suggest people 'wanted' war?

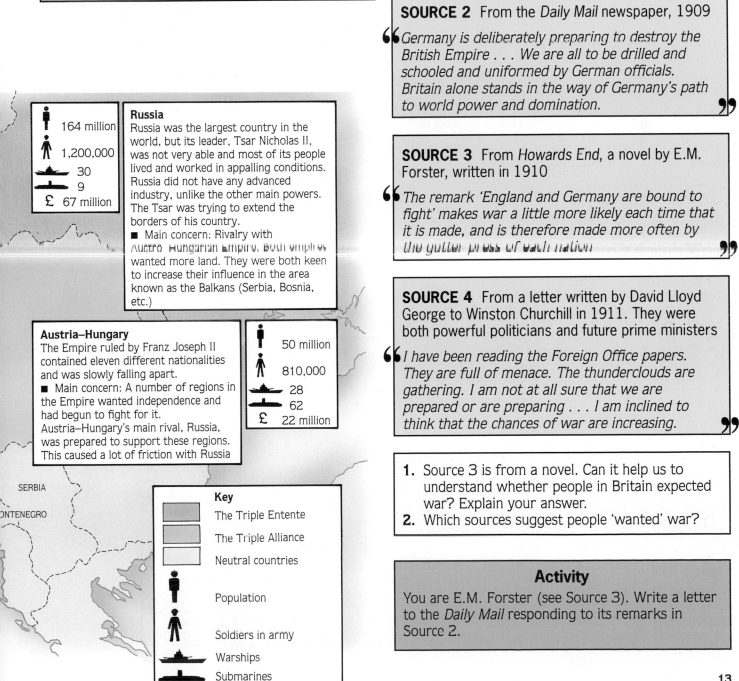

Russia
Russia was the largest country in the world, but its leader, Tsar Nicholas II, was not very able and most of its people lived and worked in appalling conditions. Russia did not have any advanced industry, unlike the other main powers. The Tsar was trying to extend the borders of his country.
■ Main concern: Rivalry with Austro-Hungarian Empire. Both empires wanted more land. They were both keen to increase their influence in the area known as the Balkans (Serbia, Bosnia, etc.)

164 million
1,200,000
30
9
£ 67 million

Austria–Hungary
The Empire ruled by Franz Joseph II contained eleven different nationalities and was slowly falling apart.
■ Main concern: A number of regions in the Empire wanted independence and had begun to fight for it.
Austria–Hungary's main rival, Russia, was prepared to support these regions. This caused a lot of friction with Russia

50 million
810,000
28
62
£ 22 million

SERBIA

ONTENEGRO

Key
The Triple Entente
The Triple Alliance
Neutral countries

Population

Soldiers in army

Warships

Submarines

£ Money spent on military preparation, 1913–14

Steps to war

BRITAIN was not the only country expecting war. Each European power had made its own plans. Many of their peoples also expected a war. It would take only a small spark to set the guns blazing.

The spark finally came in June 1914. In Sarajevo, in the state of Bosnia, the heir to the Austrian throne was assassinated by a young student, Gavrilo Princip. This set off a chain reaction throughout Europe.

23 · 28 29 30 · 1 2 3 4 · 6

July 1914   August 1914

28 June
The heir to the Austrian throne, Archduke Franz Ferdinand, is assassinated in Bosnia

The Russian army gets ready to help Serbia defend itself against the Austrian attack

To complete the picture Austria declares war on Russia

Germany sends a demand to Russia ordering it to hold back from helping Serbia

Austria declares war on Serbia. Belgrade (in Serbia) is shelled

Germany declares war on France and invades NEUTRAL Belgium. Britain orders Germany to withdraw from Belgium

BRITISH GOVERNMENT DEMANDS GERMANS LEAVE BELGIUM

The Germans are still in Belgium. Britain declares war on Germany

BRITAIN DECLARES WAR ON GERMANY

Germany declares war on Russia. It also begins to move its army towards France and Belgium

BRITAIN
GERMANY
FRANCE
AUSTRIA-HUNGARY

Austria blames Serbia for the killing of Archduke Ferdinand

It's Serbia that is behind this!

The Serbians trained those Bosnian assassins.

The French army is put on a war footing ready to fight any German invasion

1. The illustrations on this page show the events between 23 July and 6 August 1914 that led to war. See if you can put them in order.

2. Divide into groups. From the following list, choose five factors which you think were the most important reasons for war breaking out.
   ■ Germany's invasion of Belgium
   ■ the increasing size of the German army and navy
   ■ the behaviour of Austria towards Serbia
   ■ Britain's rivalry with Germany
   ■ France's desire for revenge
   ■ Germany's fear of being surrounded by France and Russia
   ■ Austria's rivalry with Russia
   ■ the size of the British Empire
   ■ Germany's desire to dominate Europe
   ■ suspicion between the main powers
   ■ the assassination of Archduke Ferdinand
   ■ the alliance system.

From your top five reasons choose one which is a long-term cause (which built up over time) and one which is a trigger. For these two say why they helped cause the War.

If the Archduke had not been shot, would a war still have broken out sooner or later?

15

Why wasn't it 'all over by Christmas'?

As you saw on page 13, anti-German feeling had been common in Britain for some time. The Germans were seen as 'the enemy'. Although there was a big protest against war a week before it broke out, once Germany invaded Belgium on 3 August many ordinary people felt that declaring war on Germany was the right thing to do. This was seen as a heroic war against 'the German aggressor'. Indeed, by 6 August most people had forgotten about the assassination of Archduke Franz Ferdinand which triggered off the conflict.

> **SOURCE 1** From a speech by David Lloyd George, the Chancellor of the Exchequer, in September 1914
>
> 66 *Belgium has been treated brutally . . . Her cornfields have been trampled down. Her villages have been destroyed. Her men have been killed and her women and children too. What had she done?*
>
> *The Germans think that we cannot beat them. It will not be easy. It will be a terrible war. But in the end we shall march through terror to triumph.* 99

Anti-war feeling evaporated almost overnight. It was replaced by fierce PATRIOTISM. Throughout Britain (and all over Europe) women cheered as husbands and sons went off to fight in Northern France. There was dancing in the streets and the queues outside the army recruitment offices were enormous.

In Germany Kaiser Wilhelm told his soldiers as they set out to fight 'You'll be home before the leaves have fallen from the trees.'

The British government warned that the War might be a terrible one, and the recruitment posters asked men to sign up 'for three years, or as long as the War lasts'. But the popular feeling was 'It will all be over by Christmas.' One soldier remembered his rush to join the army: 'Our one great fear was that the War would be over before we got there.'

What was planned

Germany and Britain had both drawn up their plans for what to do if war started (see Source 2).

SOURCE 2 A map showing what was meant to happen

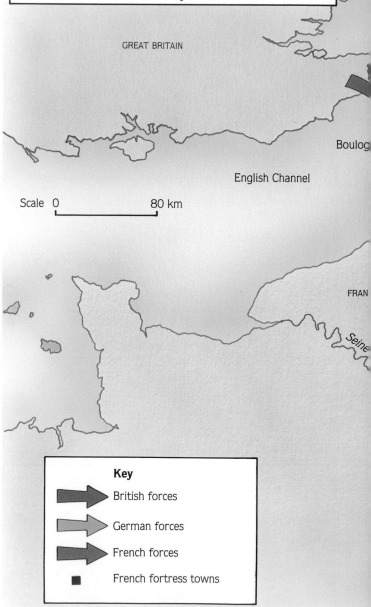

> **Stage 2: the British plan**
> The British plan was to send a small but well trained army (the British Expeditionary Force or BEF) over the Channel to help defend the French and the Belgians.
> Although the Schlieffen Plan was supposed to be a German secret the British expected the Germans to invade through Belgium. If war was declared the BEF would quickly cross to France, take the west flank alongside the French, and halt the German advance.
> The Germans would then be exposed to the east and the west; the Russians, French and British would so greatly outnumber the Germans that they would surrender

GREAT BRITAIN

Boulog

English Channel

Scale 0   80 km

FRAN

Seine

Key

→ British forces

→ German forces

→ French forces

■ French fortress towns

Stage 1: the German plan

The German plan (named the Schlieffen Plan after the German field marshal who devised it) was to invade France through NEUTRAL Belgium.

Most of the French army was on the border with Germany. The Germans thought that if they moved fast enough they could race past the French troops and capture Paris within six weeks. The war on the WESTERN FRONT would be won.

The German leaders didn't fear the small British army and they didn't really expect the British to come to the aid of the Belgians. Even if they did, the German plan was to capture the ports on the Channel – Ostend, Dunkirk, Calais and Boulogne – as they swept south. This would prevent the British army getting across to France in large numbers.

The Germans did not expect the Russians to get organised very quickly. They thought the Russians would take at least six weeks to get their army organised, so they intended to ignore them to start with. With France conquered and the British unable to land, the enormous German army could then transfer to the Eastern Front to deal with the Russians

WHY WASN'T IT 'ALL OVER BY CHRISTMAS'?

What actually happened

The Belgians fought so bravely that the German advance was slowed down. Instead of getting to Paris in six weeks, the German army was still fighting in Belgium weeks after it invaded

SOURCE 3 Stage 1: the Germans get stuck in Belgium

The Russians got their army into action much more quickly than the Germans had expected. In ten days Russian troops entered Germany. The Germans had to weaken their western armies and transfer troops to the east to prevent the Russians getting any further

As the Germans expected, the French counter-attacked in Alsace and Lorraine. They were well beaten by the Germans

The 100,000 men of the British Expeditionary Force were well trained and well equipped. They were ready for action in less than a week – far more quickly than the Germans expected. They fought with the German army at the places shown on the map. The cost was high – by December 1914, more than half of the original BEF were dead – but the western German armies abandoned hope of surrounding Paris

SOURCE 4 Stage 2: the Battle of the Marne

Just in time the French responded to the threat of the Germans' attack through Belgium. They switched troops to their border with Belgium and slowed down the advance of the main German army. Reserve troops were rushed out of Paris – some by taxi – when Paris itself was threatened. French soldiers were ordered: 'A unit which can no longer advance must at all costs retain the ground it has gained, and rather than retire, be killed on the spot.'

Key (Source 3)
- British forces
- German forces
- French forces
- ■ Fortress towns

Key (Source 4)
- British attack
- British retreat
- German attack
- German retreat
- French forces
- ■ Fortress towns
- ✗ Main battles

1. List three differences between the plan devised by Schlieffen and what actually happened.
2. Draw a diagram like the one here to show why the Schlieffen Plan failed.

'Why did the Schlieffen Plan fail?'

The war in France and Belgium was planned as 'a war of movement'. The rival armies would manoeuver, trying to outflank or trap their opponents.

By Christmas 1914, however, it was clear that neither side was going to win the quick victory each had predicted to its people. The Schlieffen Plan had failed. Secretly Crown Prince Wilhelm of Germany said, 'We have lost the War. It will go on for a long time but it is already lost.'

Even so, the Germans showed no sign of giving up. And they were strong enough to resist any counter-attack. No one could deliver the knockout blow.

The war of movement had been replaced by a STALEMATE. On the Western Front more than two million soldiers were now involved in the War. As the weather got colder and wetter they faced each other over miles of increasingly muddy land, churned up by SHELL fire. Both sides began to dig more permanent trenches to protect themselves from enemy machine gun fire.

By Christmas 1914 a long line of trenches stretched from the English Channel to the Swiss border. These trenches were to be 'home' for the soldiers of both sides for the next three years. Despite millions of casualties, neither army would move more than ten miles forwards or backwards until well into 1918.

The Germans' only hope was to surround the British and French. They swept round to the north, but the French did the same and neither side was able to trap the other. Meanwhile, the British also headed north to prevent the Germans capturing vital Channel ports such as Calais and Boulogne. They arrived just in time, helped by the Belgians, who delayed the Germans by flooding their land

SOURCE 5 Stage 3: the race for the sea

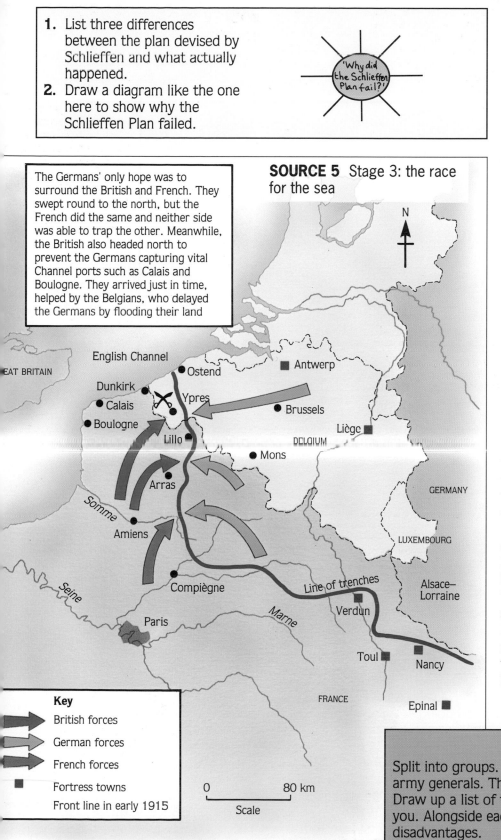

Key
- British forces
- German forces
- French forces
- ■ Fortress towns
- Front line in early 1915

0   80 km
Scale

Activity

Split into groups. You are either British or German army generals. The War has reached a stalemate. Draw up a list of the options that are available to you. Alongside each option list its advantages and disadvantages.

The Western Front: the view from Britain

WHEN war broke out the government had most of Britain on its side. Even the SUFFRAGETTES and the strikers stopped their protests and helped the war effort. When the government asked for 100,000 volunteer soldiers the response was far better than anyone expected – 750,000 men joined the army in one month.

The public were quickly deluged with PROPAGANDA, including pamphlets, posters, newspaper reports and advertisements. These showed that the War was a just war, that Germany was evil, that Britain would beat Germany, and that soldiers would feel proud to have been part of it.

---

1. Explain as carefully as you can how each poster in Source 1 is trying to persuade men to join up. Are they all using the same methods?
2. Explain why none of these posters show the conditions on the Western Front.
3. Design your own poster to persuade young men to join the army in 1914.

The propaganda deliberately did not show what was actually happening on the Western Front. Neither the new soldiers nor their families knew the horrors of the War that were awaiting them across the Channel. The recruiting posters and government propaganda gave the impression that a soldier's life was heroic, adventurous and rather romantic. In 1914 this was fairly easy as it was still mainly professional soldiers who were doing the fighting, and casualties among the volunteers remained low. As the years went on and casualties

SOURCE 1 Recruiting posters published by the government between 1914 and 1916

mounted it was more and more important that people had a positive view of what the soldiers were doing in France.

More and more soldiers were needed, so the government had to persuade men to join up. They also had to persuade parents, wives and girlfriends that the War was worthwhile and that it was a great adventure rather than a dreadful reality.

Lord Kitchener was Secretary for War in the government in 1914. He had the job of persuading men to sign up. He organised a poster campaign, and 54 million posters were issued. By 1916 over two million men had volunteered.

The government was not the only organisation trying to give a heroic impression of the War, as you can see from Sources 2–5.

SOURCE 2 A poem published in the *Daily Mail* on 12 July 1916. It describes the incident shown in Source 4, which happened on the first day of the Battle of the Somme

On through the hail of slaughter
Where gallant comrades fall,
Where blood is poured like water
They drive the trickling ball.
The fear of death before them
Is but an empty name;
True to the land that bore them
The Surreys play the game!

▼**SOURCE 3** 'Time for one more' – a cigarette advertisement

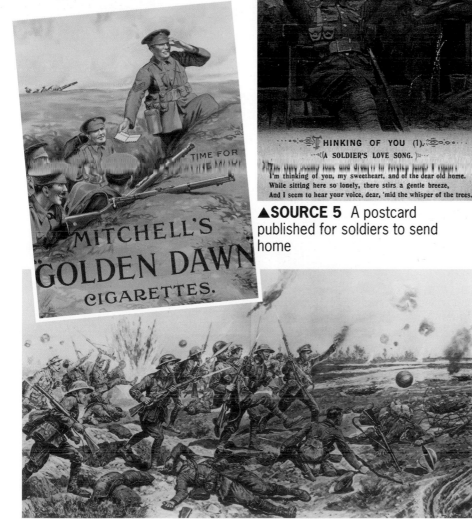

TIME FOR

MITCHELL'S
GOLDEN DAWN
CIGARETTES.

THINKING OF YOU (1).
(A SOLDIER'S LOVE SONG.)

I'm thinking of you, my sweetheart, and of the dear old home.
While sitting here so lonely, there stirs a gentle breeze,
And I seem to hear your voice, dear, 'mid the whisper of the trees.

▲**SOURCE 5** A postcard published for soldiers to send home

▲**SOURCE 4** A picture from the *Illustrated London News* of 29 July 1916 entitled *The Surreys Play the Game*. It shows men from the East Surrey Regiment kicking a football as they launch an attack

4. Look at Sources 1–5. Choose three words from this list to describe the soldiers shown in these sources: cowardly, brave, frightened, heroic, relaxed, stupid, suffering, happy. Explain why you have chosen your three words.
5. You are eighteen years old in 1914. You have spent all your life in a small village, where you have been bored. You want some adventure, you want your parents to be proud of you, and you want to see the world. Use Sources 1–5 to explain why you are joining the army.

The newspapers regularly ran optimistic reports of how the War was going. But there was no way for people to check how accurate these reports were. Letters from soldiers in France were strictly CENSORED. Newspapers themselves were censored from 1915 onwards.

Throughout the War there was a strict rule that no photographs could be published that showed a dead British soldier. Following a major battle casualty lists were sometimes not made public for weeks. And according to the editor of the *Daily Express* the newspapers chose not to focus on casualty stories. He wrote in his diary on 24 October 1914, 'The first eight or ten casualties had as much publicity as the rest put together.'

Activity

Write out a conversation that might take place between a mother and her son who is leaving for the Western Front. The conversation should describe their attitudes and feelings towards the War. Make sure you include what they think the fighting is going to be like.

What was life really like on the Western Front?

MOST people in Britain had a very inaccurate view of what soldiers were going to meet when they crossed the sea to France.

There were over two million men in the British army. Most of them served on the WESTERN FRONT. Each of these soldiers was a unique individual. His experience of going to war was different from every other soldier's. We are going to use the soldiers' own letters, diaries and poems, as well as official photographs and documents of the time, to try to reconstruct life on the Western Front.

Anyone between the ages of nineteen and 41 could volunteer, although there are plenty of stories of teenagers and older men lying about their age in order to join the army. The soldiers were drawn from all classes of society and from all regions of Britain and its Empire. A large part of Britain's army in the battles in the Middle East was made up of Indian soldiers. Some Indians, as well as Canadians, West Indians, Australians and New Zealanders, also fought on the Western Front in France.

Kitting out and training

There were so many volunteers that many of them had to wait weeks or months for equipment. They DRILLED with wooden sticks in place of real rifles.

Some of the training was very hard – ten hours a day of hard physical effort. Some of it was next to useless (see Source 1).

SOURCE 1 Written by a soldier, Gerald Brenan

For three mornings we marched about on the parade ground . . . We were not taught how to fight in trenches. These we were told were only temporary.

---

1. Look at Sources 2 and 3. How many of the items mentioned in Source 3 can you see on the soldier in Source 2?
2. Using Sources 2 and 3, draw a picture of a soldier and label his equipment.
3. Is there anything in Source 2 that suggests that the photograph was staged?

▶ **SOURCE 2** A photograph of a soldier leaving for France

SOURCE 3 List of the kit a British soldier carried with him into the trenches in 1915. The total weight was 30 kilos

■ Mark II Lee Enfield Rifle
■ large canvas pack for carrying woolly cap, spare socks and greatcoat
■ digging tool – handle and head separate
■ haversack for carrying rations, paybook, toothbrush, soap and towel, spare bootlaces, mess tin [to eat from] and cover, fork and spoon, mending and darning kit
■ full water bottle and carrier
■ bayonet [a blade that could be attached to the end of the rifle]
■ 150 rounds of ammunition in belt and pouches
■ identity tag
■ two canvas bags to carry a respirator and a gas mask
■ service cap and regimental cap badge.

Arrival in France

Most volunteers were in a Battalion or County Regiment of 1000 men. A Regiment was split up into smaller units of a Company (240 men), a Platoon (60 men) or a Section (fourteen men). Most volunteer soldiers could expect to be serving with men from their own home area, or even with friends from before the War. They often served in 'Pals' Regiments' such as 'The Bradford Lads' or 'The Derby Lads'. These friendships helped support many soldiers through the boredom and the horrors of trench warfare.

They travelled over to France – usually by night – in open topped boats. Early in the War there was little risk of being attacked by German U-boats (submarines). They landed at Channel ports such as Le Havre.

Once in France the soldier would not usually be sent to the FRONT LINE straight away. He would live in a temporary camp or a COMMANDEERED building for further training and preparation.

SOURCE 4 Written in 1973 by the novelist Henry Williamson, who went to France in 1914

6 *We landed at Le Havre and after one night in a rest camp found ourselves in a series of trucks.*

At St Omer we marched to a convent, where we practised advances in formation across old stubble, and rumours said we were 'for it'. That night six of us stood among the trees of the garden and watched flickerings in the faraway eastern sky and heard the boom of heavy guns.

Next morning we marched north along a straight road between rows of elms and so to Wipers [the British soldiers' name for Ypres]. We slept that night in the cloth hall.

In the morning the bugles sounded the alarm . . . Up the Menin Road we marched when coming towards us were prams holding silent children, wounded soldiers, refugees with sacks filled with dead chickens and 40 tall soldiers with staring eyes and hollow cheeks.

We were not needed [at the front] and returned to Ypres . . . and marching south found ourselves in a large wood of oaks. There we remained interested and content for the weather was warm. We slept in bunkers made of oak posts and sand bags. 99

SOURCE 5 From the autobiography of Gerald Brenan, published in 1968

6 *In March 1915, we found ourselves in billets in a farmhouse near Armentières on the Belgian frontier. The country around us was green and lush, with more civilians than soldiers. In contrast with this was the continual sound of the guns.*

A few days later, my company had a short spell in the trenches near Messines . . . As I stood looking at the German lines, the sentry next to me was shot in the head and fell back dead. But I was too excited by the novelty of everything to be affected by this, my first sight of death. I was young and full of life – it could not happen to me. 99

1. Do you think it is a good idea that soldiers serve with people from their own home area?
2. Look at Sources 4 and 5. What were Henry Williamson's and Gerald Brenan's reactions to their first sight of war?

SOURCE 6 The Worcestershire Regiment going into action – a photograph taken on 28 June 1916

SOURCE 7 The road from Menin to Ypres, the main route to the front-line trenches at Ypres, in 1917

Up to the front line

The FRONT LINE was made up of trenches which stretched for hundreds of kilometres, from the coast of Belgium to the border of Switzerland. The soldiers were sent up to the front line for various reasons: in preparation for an attack, to defend against a German attack, or to keep the trenches repaired. Each company was supposed to spend a maximum of six days per month in the front-line trenches, but in practice many soldiers could spend months at a time there – if they survived.

The front-line trenches were backed up by support trenches, communication trenches, dead-end trenches (to confuse the enemy) and large DUGOUTS.

The area between the two sides was known as 'No Man's Land'. Any attack across this area would be slowed down by yards of barbed wire and by the murderous fire from machine gun posts which could wipe out a whole company in minutes.

Key
1 Front line
2 Enemy front line
3 No Man's Land
4 Support trenches
5 Dead end
6 Barbed wire
7 Communication trenches

SOURCE 8 The trench system

Activity

The view from the trenches

Draw a large circle on a piece of plain card. This is the lens of a periscope, through which you are looking at the German lines across 'No Man's Land'. Use the evidence to draw inside the circle what you might see through the lens.

You could also draw a poppy around the 'lens' (as on the front cover of this book) to make an effective symbol of the War on the Western Front. Use the views to make a classroom display.

1. Copy Source 8 into your book and number the features correctly using the key. Mark German trenches in one colour and British trenches in another colour.
2. Why do you think the trenches were designed in a zig-zag pattern?
3. On your own copy of Source 8 show the route a platoon of soldiers could take to make their way from x to y on the plan.

SOURCE 9 An artist's view of a trench

Life in the trenches

SOURCE 10 From a children's comic of 1992

1. This comic would not claim to be a serious piece of history, but do you think it might be able to give us an accurate picture of life in the trenches? Make a list of things that you think are likely to be accurate/inaccurate in Source 10. Then compare your ideas with the information in Sources 11–19 over the page.

SOURCE 11 A British soldier made this list of daily rations in his notebook

> | Bully (corned) beef | 1lb. [454g] |
> | Bread or biscuits | 1¼lbs [567g] |
> | Bacon | ¼lb. [113g] |
> | Tea | ½oz. [14g] |
> | Sugar | 2oz. [56g] |
> | Jam | 2oz. [56g] |
> | Cheese | 1oz. [28g] |
> | Butter | ¾oz. [21g] |
> | Potatoes | ¾lb. [340g] |
>
> Also: small amounts of salt, pepper and mustard.

SOURCE 12 Mealtime for the front-line troops at a field kitchen in October 1916

1. Is the soldier in Source 11 well fed?
2. Many soldiers complained about their food, especially once they were sent up to the front-line trenches. Why do you think they complained?

For the soldiers in the trenches the mood varied between discomfort, boredom, anxiety and uncertainty.

The soldiers' life was greatly affected by the weather. In rain their trenches could be knee-deep in water. In winter the mud could freeze as hard as rock. In summer it could bake in blistering heat.

For much of the time shells were falling, so working, sleeping or eating the soldiers had to live with the fear of being killed by an exploding shell.

The front-line trenches were most active at night. An attack was always most likely at night, so sentries had to keep a careful watch, while others repaired defences or barbed wire, or carried out scouting and spying missions.

Despite the constant dangers of trench life, the daytime was mostly very boring. Some soldiers tried to sleep. Others just sat around reading, or smoking, or playing cards. There were also routine jobs to do, such as filling sandbags, cleaning latrines and fetching supplies.

3. Each of the written sources on pages 26–27 describes a problem facing the soldiers. Put a heading in your book which you think best describes the problem, e.g. Source 13 could be 'Water' or 'Animals'. Underneath each heading, explain what the problem was, and how it affected the soldiers.

SOURCE 13 A journalist's view of trenches during the Battle of the Somme

> The water in the trenches through which we waded was alive with a multitude of swimming frogs. Red slugs crawled up the side of the trenches and strange beetles with dangerous looking horns wriggled along dry ledges and invaded the dugouts, in search of the lice which infested them.

SOURCE 14 By Sergeant Harry Roberts, who lived in a flooded trench for six days

> If you have never had trench feet described to you, I will explain. Your feet swell to two or three times their normal size and go completely dead. You could stick a bayonet into them and not feel a thing.
>
> If you are lucky enough not to lose your feet and the swelling begins to go down, it is then that the indescribable agony begins. I have heard men cry and scream with the pain and many have had to have their feet and legs amputated.
>
> I was one of the lucky ones, but one more day in that trench and it may have been too late.

SOURCE 15 The last letter from Private Peter MacGregor to his wife in September 1916. He was killed shortly afterwards by a direct hit on his trench by an enemy shell

I am well and looking forward to the end of the War. I wish it would hurry up.

One of our men was caught by a sniper – he was standing at the entrance to his dugout, the bullet went in under his shoulder – alas, alas.

When I was standing at the cookhouse door, I saw the stretcher which came along to take the poor fellow away – how sad it was, he was carried out, wrapped up in his waterproof sheet, placed in this thing and whisked away.

The business of the hour has to go on. A dead man is no use to the army, get him out of the way as quickly as possible. War is a terrible thing and so few people realise it.

SOURCE 16 From *Goodbye to All That*, the novelist Robert Graves' account of his experiences during the War

To get a 'cushy' one [an injury bad enough to get you sent home] is all the old hands think about.

Bloke in the Camerons wanted a 'cushy', bad! Fed up and far from home he was. He puts his hand over the top and gets a trigger finger taken off, and two more besides. 'I'm off to bonny Scotland!' he says, laughing. But on the way down the trench to the dressing station [where wounds were treated], he forgets to stoop low where the old sniper's working. He gets it through the head.

SOURCE 17 An official account of a court martial (a military trial) in 1916. This soldier had been one of the first to enlist in 1914

No 1 . . . 2 Private A . . . B . . . the Battalion (Pioneers) South Staffordshire Regiment was tried by FGCM on the following charge: 'Misbehaving in such a manner as to show cowardice.' The accused, when proceeding with a party for work in the trenches, ran away owing to the bursting of a shell and did not afterwards rejoin the party.

The sentence of the court was 'to suffer death by being shot'. The sentence was duly carried out at 5.50 a.m. on 18 October 1916.

SOURCE 18 From an interview with driver R.L. Venables

Whilst asleep during the night, we were frequently awakened by rats running over us. When this happened too often for my liking, I would lie on my back and wait for a rat to linger on my legs; then violently heave my legs upward, throwing the rat into the air. Occasionally, I would hear a grunt when the rat landed on a fellow victim.

SOURCE 19 A British trench photographed in 1916

The soldiers faced all these problems before they had even seen a German. The worst was yet to come.

4. The soldiers in Sources 16 and 17 tried to get away from the fighting. Which one do you have most sympathy with and why?
5. Why do you think the soldier in Source 17 was executed?
6. Now that you have studied these sources about life in the trenches, how accurate do you think Source 10 is?
7. Do you think the fact that the artist of Source 10 was drawing for a children's comic influenced the kind of pictures he drew?

Preparations for attack

There was no way of getting round the ends of your enemy's trenches, so the only means of attacking the enemy was through a full-frontal attack – charging at the enemy trenches. The generals were convinced that if they could only get enough soldiers 'over the top', charging in a human wave, then they would break through the enemy defences and capture their trenches. Throughout 1915, full-frontal attacks were launched to try to break the deadlock. Battles at Neuve Chapelle, Compiègne, Ypres, Arras and Loos resulted in the British and the ALLIES losing nearly 400,000 dead for a gain in territory of about ten square kilometres. This was trench warfare!

Whenever a major attack was planned, there was ground or aircraft RECONNAISSANCE to check out the enemy position. The soldiers were informed well beforehand. Before the attack there were massive ARTILLERY BOMBARDMENTS, which were aimed to weaken the enemy defences but which would also warn the enemy that an attack was on its way.

When the whistle sounded, often at dawn, the soldiers began the advance across 'No Man's Land' towards the German lines. They knew the chances of survival were slim, and they realised that many of these attacks were totally pointless and rarely gained anything worthwhile, but orders had to be obeyed.

SOURCE 20 From A.P. Herbert's war novel *The Secret Battle*, published in 1919. The author served as a soldier on the Western Front. In this extract plans are being laid for an attack on the enemy trenches

There was a theory that this particular section of enemy trench had been evacuated . . . Harry was told to get right up to that trench, to look in, and see what was in it. It was a thing he had done twice before . . . It meant the usual breathless, toilsome wriggle across No Man's Land, avoiding the flares and the two snipers who covered that bit of the ground, finding a gap in the wires, getting through without being seen, without noise, without catching his clothes on a wandering barb, or banging his revolver against a multitude of tin cans. Then you had to listen and wait and if possible look in the trench.

When (and if) you had done that you had to get back . . . past the same obstacles, the same snipers.

However, Harry was a scout and it was his job.

SOURCE 21 From *Goodbye to All That*, by the novelist Robert Graves

On 19 September 1915, we relieved the Middlesex Regiment at Cambrin and were told that these would be the trenches from which we attacked.

The bombardment had already started a week in advance . . . The trenches shook and a great cloud of drifting shell-smoke hid the German lines. Shells went over our heads in a steady stream; we had to shout to make our neighbours hear.

Dying down a little at night, the racket began every morning at dawn . . . More casualties came from our 'shorts' and 'blow-backs' [British shells which landed close to British trenches] than from German shells. I got two small wounds on the hand.

SOURCE 22 Written by a photographer, Geoffrey Malins, who was sent to France by the government to photograph the Battle of the Somme. He is describing the night before the start of the Battle of the Somme

Crowds of men were crouching round, heating up their canteens of water, some frying pieces of meat, others heating soup, and all the time laughing and talking. From other groups came the quiet humming of favourite songs . . . And these men knew they were going over the top in the morning. They knew that many would not be alive tomorrow night, yet I never saw a sad face, nor heard a word of complaint . . .

Over the top

SOURCE 23 These are stills from an official British film made in 1916. Some historians think this was a staged event

SOURCE 24 Crawling to the German trenches under fire – this photograph was taken on a training exercise

SOURCE 25 Written by Private Henry Russell about the Battle of the Somme in 1916

" *During our advance, I saw many of my colleagues killed by German machine gun fire, but this somehow or other did not seem to worry me and I continued to go forward until I suddenly became aware that there were few of us left capable of going on.*

I found myself in the company of an officer, Lieutenant Wallace. We dived into a flat, shallow hole made by our guns, not knowing what to do next . . . I came to the conclusion that going on would be suicidal and that the best thing we could do would be to stay there and try to pick off any Germans who might expose themselves. Lieut. Wallace said, however, that we had been ordered to go on at all costs and that we must comply with this order. At this, he stood up and within a few seconds dropped down riddled with bullets. This left me with the same problem and having observed his action, I felt that I must do the same. I stood up and was immediately hit by two bullets and dropped down . . .

I am now convinced that when it comes to the crunch, nobody has any fear at all. "

Activity

Write a diary for a period of one week in November 1915, starting on a Monday. Your diary could include information from any of the sources in this section or from previous sections. It should include details about trench conditions and an attack when you went 'over the top'.

The aftermath

During the War almost a million soldiers of the British Empire were killed. Germany and Russia each lost nearly two million dead, France and Austria–Hungary each lost a million and a half and Italy half a million. It was the machine guns on both sides that accounted for most of the dead. It may seem suicidal to have kept on sending troops across 'No Man's Land', but throughout the years 1914 to 1917 those were the tactics used by the generals from HQ (headquarters), far behind the front lines. Little was gained during this time.

SOURCE 26 Casualties of the Battle of the Somme

But orders had to be obeyed and it was only very rarely that soldiers refused. There was a serious mutiny in the French army in April 1917 which led to 55 soldiers being executed. In September 1917 there was a riot by several thousand British and Commonwealth soldiers at the Army Base Camp in Etaples, but most historians see this as a protest against conditions rather than an anti-war protest. In the whole War 332 British soldiers were executed for offences such as cowardice (see Source 17 on page 27).

---

1. Sources 20–26 include extracts from novels, eye-witness reports, staged photographs and real life photographs. Make a list of the problems involved in using each type of evidence to understand what it was like to be involved in an attack on the German trenches.

Behind the lines

Wounded soldiers often depended on the bravery of their mates, who would have to carry them back to their own trenches. Many of the wounded died in 'No Man's Land' because there was no one to help them. But the lucky ones would be carried back to makeshift hospitals and DRESSING STATIONS behind the lines – beyond the reach of the machine guns and shells.

There were many soldiers and support workers working behind the lines. This was where the War was run. This was where thousands of casualties were cared for. This was where supplies of weapons, food, medicines and clothes were stored and organised for the whole British Army. This was where most of the women who had enlisted in the Voluntary Aid Detachments (VAD) – a nursing group – and the First Aid Nursing Auxiliary (FANY) were working.

SOURCE 27 Victims of poison gas at a dressing station

SOURCE 28 Mairi Chisholm and Elizabeth, Baroness de T'Serclaes driving an ambulance through the ruins of the French town of Pervyse in 1917. Both had joined FANY

Some men saw a job behind the lines as a 'cushy' (easy) option. As the War progressed and more manpower was needed in the fighting lines, womanpower became more and more important in the support services behind the lines. In 1917 12,000 men were working behind the lines in France. The generals decided that women should do most of these jobs: cooking, cleaning, typing letters and official documents, and medical duties. So in 1917 the Women's Army Auxiliary Corps (WAAC) was set up as a separate army unit, serving in difficult and dangerous conditions. The women had no special privileges and suffered the same hardships as the men they replaced.

> **SOURCE 29** From Elizabeth de T'Serclaes' autobiography
>
> 66 *We slept in our clothes and cut our hair short so that it would tuck inside our caps. Dressing meant simply putting on our boots . . . There were times when we had to scrape the lice off with the blunt edge of a knife and our underclothes stuck to us.* 99

> **SOURCE 30** From a book about women in the War by a modern historian, Roy Terry
>
> 66 *On 30 May 1918, eight women were killed in a raid on Camp 1 at Abbeville in Northern France. Seven others were wounded, one of whom died later. The bravery of the survivors earned commendations from all and three military medals were awarded to the women who helped in the rescue . . .*
>
> *Up to this time, the only women killed had been hospital personnel, and newspaper reporters were keen to have a go at the enemy for killing women . . . However, it was pointed out that because the women were replacing combatants, the enemy could be excused for killing them if he could.* 99

1. Make a list of all the types of work that women did in support of the front-line troops.
2. What was the main reason for the setting up of the WAAC?
3. What does this tell you about attitudes towards women at the time?
4. How important do you think women's support role was?

Activity

Between 1916 and 1918 the soldiers of the 12th Battalion the Sherwood Foresters produced a trench newspaper called the *Wipers Times*. It was not the only trench newspaper, but it was the only one produced at the front by the soldiers who were engaged in the fighting.

To start with the newspaper was printed on an old printing press the soldiers had found in a bombed out building in Ypres.

The *Wipers Times* contained poems, letters, stories, advertisements and comments on the fighting. It was mostly humorous – even the dreadful battles were treated with humour.

Get into groups. It is your job to produce an issue of the *Wipers Times*. You can use some of the pieces you have produced over the past few pages, or write new ones. Your teacher will give you a design for the head of your newspaper.

Back home again

Some wounded soldiers recovered behind the lines. Others were sent back to Britain. There were those with shell-shock – a kind of nervous breakdown brought on by the War. There were those who'd been blinded or had their lungs corroded by a poison gas attack. There were those who had lost legs, feet or hands, or been badly burned. Boats regularly crossed the Channel taking the sick and even the dying back to Britain.

Healthy soldiers went home too, on LEAVE. Some soldiers went home on official duties.

Each of them carried with him his own memories of the experiences of War. Now they faced a new problem – what to say to their family and friends about the horrors of the War on the Western Front.

Activity

Work in fours. One of you is a soldier who has just come home on leave. The rest of you are his family. His father asks: 'So, son. Tell us what it was like out there.'

What happens next?

Coming home

FOR the soldier returning from the trenches on LEAVE England was a longed-for haven. Yet many of them did not actually enjoy their time back in 'Blighty'. The terrible experiences they had been through set them apart from people in Britain. One CIVILIAN described the returning soldiers as 'like strange beings from another world . . . stained with the mud of the trenches.' To the soldier Britain also seemed strange, with everybody so enthusiastic about the War. You can read what one soldier felt in Source 1.

SOURCE 1 A description of the thoughts of a wounded soldier back in England by the historian R.H. Tawney, who was wounded during the Battle of the Somme

" *The Tommy [soldier] we read about in the magazines is a creature at once ridiculous and disgusting. He is shown as 'cheerful' and enjoying the 'excitement' of war, of finding 'sport' in killing other men, or hunting Germans out of dugouts as a terrier hunts rats.*

Of the soldier's internal life, the sensation of taking part in a game played by monkeys and organised by lunatics, you realise, I think, nothing. "

The cartoons on this page bring together the experiences of four different soldiers.

1. Try to explain why each soldier in the cartoons finds it difficult to make people understand what the War is really like.
2. Have you any advice for each of the soldiers?

32

They don't understand. They make it sound like I'm on holiday.

3 Government says we farm workers are as important to the War as you lot out there.

So they see we are looked after.

More than they do for us.

4 You never tell me what it's like out there. You should talk about it. You'd feel better.

Some things it's better you shouldn't know.

6

7 'You walk along the trenches... The day is fine, and men are asleep, basking like cats, on sunny little shelves and bunks cunningly sculptured out of the trenches firm clay walls.'

Why don't you print the real stories – I could tell you.

That's a wonderful book. It really helped me imagine what it's like for you soldiers out in the trenches.

WESTERN FRONT
DRAWINGS BY MUIRHEAD BONE

8 <u>Atrocities</u>
'You bragged how once your men in savage mood
Butchered some Saxon prisoners. That was good!
I trust you felt no pity when they stood
Patient and cowed and scared, as prisoners should.

How did you kill them? Speak and don't be shy:
You know I love to hear how Germans die,
. . . . .'

This was too much for my publishers!

REJECT

REJECTS

SASSOON POEMS
SIEGFRIED SASSOON

Images and impressions of war

MEN from all walks of life joined the army, and among them were many artists. There was even a regiment called 'The Artists' Rifles'. The government realised how valuable these artists could be to its PROPAGANDA campaign. The Ministry of Information – which was in charge of propaganda – thought war artists would be particularly useful for convincing NEUTRAL countries, such as the USA, either to stay neutral or, better still, to join the War on the ALLIES' side. They therefore employed official war artists to record scenes from the War. The main restriction on the artists was that no picture could be displayed which showed a dead British soldier.

Pictures by official war artists, such as those in Sources 1–5, were used to illustrate books and pamphlets put out by the government. They were also shown in exhibitions all around the country.

---

1. If you were trying to convince the USA to join the War on the Allies' side what kind of pictures would you want to be able to show them?

▶ **SOURCE 2** *Over the Top* by John Nash (1893–1977).He was Paul Nash's younger brother. He joined the army in September 1916. He served in France from November 1916 to January 1918, when he was made an official war artist

▲**SOURCE 3** *Paths of Glory* by C.R.W. Nevinson (1889–1946). He joined the Red Cross in 1914, working as a driver, interpreter and stretcher-bearer in France, and with the Army Medical Corps at a hospital in London. His own health was ruined by the War and he was invalided out in January 1916. He exhibited some of his war paintings in London in September 1916, and was made a war artist in 1917. He was sent to France for the early weeks of the Battle of Passchendaele. This picture was painted in 1917, but not exhibited until after the War because of the ban on showing dead British soldiers

▶ **SOURCE 1** *The Menin Road* by Paul Nash (1889–1946). He joined up in 1914, and served at Ypres in 1916. While wounded in 1917 he painted more than 60 paintings in eight weeks for an exhibition in London. The government was so impressed with his pictures that they made him an official war artist in November 1917. This picture shows the road out of Ypres

SOURCE 4 *The Machine Gunners* by C.R.W. Nevinson (see Source 3)

SOURCE 5 *Gassed* by John Singer Sargent (1856–1925) He was aged 60 when the government sent him to France in 1918 to paint a picture to symbolise the co-operation of the British and the Americans. He quickly abandoned his official project, and painted instead the scenes he saw behind the lines – including this clearing station for casualties of a mustard gas attack

2. Choose one of the paintings in Sources 1–5 and write a paragraph about what you can see in the painting.

3. Elsewhere in this book there are photographs showing similar places and events to those in Sources 1–5. Look up Source 7 on page 46, Source 23 on page 29, Source 27 on page 30, Source 7 on page 23 and Source 26 on page 30 and match them to Sources 1–5.

4. Compare the painting you wrote about for question 2 with the photograph of the same subject. Does it give the same impression or a different impression of that aspect of the War?

5. All the painters and photographers experienced the War at first hand. Which type of evidence – photos or paintings – would you consider to be:
   a) the most reliable record of the War
   b) the most useful for showing what the War was really like?

6. Why do you think the government wanted painters to record the War as well as photographers?

Activity

You have been invited to select photos and paintings for an exhibition on the First World War. You can choose paintings or photos from anywhere in this book.
1. Which three will you choose to show how terrible the War was?
2. Which three will you choose to show how heroic the War was?

Poetry

Thousands of words of poetry were written during the First World War. You have already seen one example (Source 2 on page 21). Some of the poetry was sentimental nonsense, but the best of it managed to put into words the compassion, the anger, the frustration, the glory and the stupidity of war, in a way that prose could not. See what you think.

> **SOURCE 6** *A Working Party* by Siegfried Sassoon (1886–1967). He served in the army for most of the War, and became increasingly angry about the way the generals were running it. This poem was written in 1917
>
> ❝ . . . *Three hours ago he stumbled up the trench*
> *Now he will never walk that road again:*
> *He must be carried back, a jolting lump*
> *Beyond all need of tenderness and care.*
>
> *He was a young man with a meagre wife*
> *And two small children in a Midland town;*
> *He showed their photographs to all his mates,*
> *And they considered him a decent chap*
> *Who did his work and hadn't much to say,*
> *And always laughed at other people's jokes*
> *Because he hadn't any of his own.*
>
> *That night when he was busy at his job*
> *Of piling bags along the parapet,*
> *He thought how slow time went, stamping his feet*
> *And blowing on his fingers, pinched with cold.*
> *He thought of getting back by half-past twelve,*
> *And tot of rum to send him warm to sleep*
> *In draughty dugout frowsty with the fumes*
> *Of coke, and full of snoring, weary men.*
>
> *He pushed another bag along the top,*
> *Craning his body outward; then a flare*
> *Gave one glimpse of No Man's Land and wire,*
> *And as he dropped his head the instant split*
> *His startled life with lead, and all went out.* ❞

> **SOURCE 7** *To My Brother (In Memory of July 1st 1916)* by Vera Brittain (1893–1970). Her brother, Captain Edward Brittain, won a Military Cross medal at the Battle of the Somme in 1916 and died on 15 June 1918, four days after the poem was written
>
> ❝ *Your battle-wounds are scars upon my heart,*
> *Received when in that grand and tragic 'show'*
>   *You played your part*
>   *Two years ago,*
>
> *And silver in the summer morning sun*
> *I see the symbol of your courage glow —*
>   *That Cross you won*
>   *Two years ago.*
>
> *Though now again you watch the shrapnel fly,*
> *And hear the guns that daily louder grow,*
>   *As in July*
>   *Two years ago,*
>
> *May you endure to lead the Last Advance,*
> *And with your men pursue the flying foe,*
>   *As once in France*
>   *Two years ago.* ❞

> **SOURCE 8** From *The Song of the Mud* by Mary Borden (1887–1968), who ran a mobile hospital at the Western Front. This poem was written in 1917
>
> ❝ *This is the hymn of mud – the obscene, the filthy, the putrid,*
> *The vast liquid grave of our armies.*
> *It has drowned our men.*
> *Its monstrous distended belly reeks with the undigested dead.*
> *Our men have gone into it, sinking slowly*
>   *And struggling and slowly disappearing*
> *Our fine men, our brave, strong, young men;* ❞

1. Source 7 could be summed up as 'A woman hopes her brave brother survives the War'; Source 6 could be summed up as 'A dull, ordinary bloke gets shot as a result of his own stupidity'. How have the poets turned their poems into more than this?

2. In Sources 9 and 11 lines have been missed out. Copy out the poems and complete them by adding lines that you think fit well.
3. Compare ideas with other people in the class. Your teacher will tell you what the poets actually wrote.

SOURCE 9 *Trench Idyll* by Richard Aldington (1892–1962). This poem was written in 1918, after he was invalided out of the army

We sat together in the trench,
He on a lump of frozen earth
Blown in the night before,
I on an unexploded shell;
And smoked and talked, like exiles,
Of ....
How at that very hour
The taxi-cabs were taking folk to dine . . .
Then we sat silent for a while
As a machine gun swept the parapet.

He said:
'I've been here on and off two years
And only seen one man killed.'

'That's odd.'

'The bullet hit him in the throat; He fell in a heap
on the fire-step,
And called out, "My God! DEAD!" '

'Good Lord, how terrible!'

'Well, as to that, the nastiest job I've had
Was last year on this very front
Taking the [identity] discs at night from men
Who'd hung for six months on the wire
Just over there.
The worst of all was
..
Thank God we couldn't see their faces;
They had gas helmets on . . .'

I shivered;
'It's rather cold here, sir, suppose we move?'

SOURCE 10 From *1914 – The Soldier* by Rupert Brooke (1887–1915). He died in Greece on his way to fight in Turkey

If I should die, think only this of me:
That there's some corner of a foreign field
That is forever England. There shall be
In that rich earth a richer dust concealed;
A dust whom England bore, shaped, made aware,
Gave, once, her flowers to love, her ways to roam,
A body of England's, breathing English air,
Washed by the rivers, blest by suns of home . . .

SOURCE 11 *In Flanders Fields* by John McCrae (1872–1918). He wrote this poem in 1915 when he was a medical officer in France

In Flanders fields the poppies blow
Between the crosses, row on row,
That mark our place; and in the sky
The larks, still bravely singing, fly
Scarce heard amid the guns below.

We are the Dead. Short days ago
We lived, felt dawn, saw sunset glow,
Loved and were loved, and now we lie
In Flanders fields.

Take up our quarrel with the foe:
To you from falling hands we throw
The torch; be yours to hold it high.
If ....
We will not sleep, though poppies grow
In Flanders fields.

SOURCE 12 From *Dulce et Decorum Est*, written in 1917 by Wilfred Owen (1893–1918). He was killed while serving on the Western Front

If in some smothering dreams you too could pace
Behind the wagon that we flung him in, . . .
If you could hear, at every jolt, the blood
Come gargling from the froth-corrupted lungs,
Obscene as cancer, bitter as the cud
Of vile, incurable sores on innocent tongues, —
My friend, you would not tell with such high zest
To children ardent for some desperate glory,
The old Lie: Dulce et decorum est Pro patria mori.
[It is sweet and proper to die for your country]

4. Do Sources 10 and 12 suggest that it is brave or stupid to die for your country? How?

Activity

Work in pairs. Choose one of the following tasks.
A. Supporters of the War have asked you to produce a poster headlined: 'Fight For Your Country'.
B. Protesters against the War have asked you to produce a poster headlined 'End the Killing'.

Choose a painting from Sources 1–5 and a phrase from Sources 6–12 to use for the poster.

Field Marshal Haig: 'the Butcher of the Somme'?

In December 1915 it was still STALEMATE on the Western Front. Neither side had made any real progress towards victory, although hundreds of attacks had been launched by either side and hundreds of thousands of soldiers killed.

The British began to question how well their army was being led, and on 10 December 1915 a new commander of the British forces was appointed. He was Field Marshal Haig. He was 54 and he had already had a long and successful military career. In particular he had been a celebrated CAVALRY commander in the Boer War fifteen years earlier. In that war the British fought against a poorly equipped enemy on the dry plains of South Africa.

Haig faced a difficult task. Trench warfare was a new kind of fighting. Some people had predicted years before the First World War that a European war would end in stalemate with each side dug into trenches. But no one really knew how to cope with trench warfare now it was here. No one knew how to win a war like this. So the generals fell back on the ideas they had used successfully in past wars.

1. Look at Source 1. Do you agree with any of Haig's ideas about warfare?
2. Do you think people at the time would have agreed or disagreed with him?
3. How do you think a) soldiers in France and b) civilians in Britain would react to the news that Haig had been appointed as the new commander?

1907 Success in battle depends mainly on morale and determination.

1915 The way to capture machine guns is by grit and determination.

1916 The machine gun is a much overrated weapon.

1916 We must wear the enemy down as much as possible.

SOURCE 1 Some of Field Marshal Haig's statements about how wars should be fought

SOURCE 2 The Western Front in February 1916

In February 1916 the Germans began yet another attack. They sent wave upon wave of soldiers over the top to attack the French forts around the town of Verdun (see Source 2). They did not expect to break through, but they did hope to wear down the morale and strength of the French soldiers. Five months and 700,000 deaths later, the French were still hanging on, but only just. The British desperately needed to relieve the pressure on the French.

So the British High Command led by Field Marshal Haig decided to begin a major attack along the line of the River Somme. They hoped this would draw German soldiers away from the attack on Verdun. Haig also hoped that a British success at the Somme would strengthen the morale of French soldiers. What's more, he had information that suggested that the Germans were outnumbered and that their morale was low.

For a week at the end of June the ARTILLERY BOMBARDMENT took place and then, finally, on 1 July 1916, the order to go over the top was given. Nearly five months later the pressure on Verdun had been lifted, but at the Somme only a few square miles of blood and mud had been gained, and hundreds of thousands of soldiers had died. On 18 November 1916, when blizzards covered the area in snow, Field Marshall Haig called a halt to the attack.

This was one of the bloodiest battles in the War. It resulted in more British dead than any battle before it. It has earned Haig the title 'the Butcher of the Somme': the man responsible for unnecessarily, almost casually, sending thousands of young British men to their deaths – for almost no gain at all.

Source 3 gives one example of attitudes to Haig. It comes from a recent BBC television series called *Blackadder Goes Forth*. For six episodes Captain Blackadder and Private Baldrick try to avoid going over the top. Their fellow soldier Lieutenant George is much more enthusiastic. The conversation takes place 'in 1916'.

> **4.** Look at Source 3. What impression of Field Marshal Haig does Blackadder give?

My instincts lead me to believe that we are at last about to go over the top.

Great Scott, Sir! You mean the moment has finally arrived for us to give Harry Hun a darn good British style thrashing, six of the best, trousers down?

You mean 'Are we all going to get killed?' Yes. Clearly Field Marshal Haig is about to make yet another giant effort to move his drinks cabinet six inches closer to Berlin.

SOURCE 3 A still from *Blackadder Goes Forth*, showing Lieutenant George on the left and Captain Blackadder on the right

On pages 40–43 we are going to consider whether Haig deserves his bad reputation. We investigate whether he was a bad commander who made mistakes or whether he was simply too ready to accept high casualties. We also consider whether he was out of touch with what was happening at the front line or whether there were simply no alternatives to the tactics he followed.

Using the evidence on these pages, you can compare Haig's statements about the Battle of the Somme with some observations by people who were at the front line.

Haig's views

> **SOURCE 4** Written by Haig in June 1916 before the battle began
>
> " *The nation must be taught to bear losses. No amount of skill on the part of the higher commanders, no training, however good, on the part of the officers and men, no superiority of arms and ammunition, however great, will enable victories to be won without the sacrifice of men's lives. The nation must be prepared to see heavy casualty lists.* "

> **SOURCE 5** Written by Haig on 30 June 1916, the day before the attack started
>
> " *The men are in splendid spirits. Several have said that they have never before been so instructed and informed of the nature of the operation before them. The barbed wire has never been so well cut, nor the artillery preparation so thorough. All the commanders are full of confidence.* "

> **SOURCE 6** From a report by Haig on the first day of the attack, 1 July 1916
>
> " *Very successful attack this morning . . . All went like clockwork . . . The battle is going very well for us and already the Germans are surrendering freely. The enemy is so short of men that he is collecting them from all parts of the line. Our troops are in wonderful spirits and full of confidence.* "

The soldiers' views

- The wire had not been cut.
- The Germans had dug trenches so deep that the bombardment had not caused much damage.
- As a general, Haig never personally visited the FRONT LINE.

> **SOURCE 7** From an interview with Private George Coppard, who survived the Battle of the Somme
>
> " *Hundreds of dead were strung out [on the barbed wire] like wreckage washed up to a high water mark. Quite as many died on the enemy wire as on the ground . . . It was clear that there were no gaps in the wire at the time of attack. The Germans must have been reinforcing the wire for months. It was so thick that daylight could barely be seen through it . . . How did the planners imagine that Tommies [British soldiers] would get through the wire? Who told them that artillery fire would pound such wire to pieces? Any Tommy could have told them that shell fire lifts wire up and drops it down, often in a worse tangle than before.* "

- There were 60,000 British casualties on the first day of the battle.
- Many German prisoners were taken.
- One Canadian battalion lost 700 out of 850 men!

> **SOURCE 8** Written in 1988 in a biography of Haig by Gerard De Groot
>
> " *While Haig slept in a cosy bed in a quiet country chateau and dined on the best food available, his men lived in muddy, noisy trenches sharing their bully beef and biscuits with big, bloated rats. It apparently did not bother Haig that his war was so much more comfortable than that of the men he commanded.* "

1. Look at Sources 4 and 5. What do you think Haig expected to happen on the first day of the fighting?
2. Why did this not happen?

SOURCE 9 The Worcestershire Regiment coming out of the trenches in September 1916, after a three-month stint during the Battle of the Somme

> 3. Which of the following statements can be supported by Sources 4–8?
>   ■ 'Haig was ignorant of what was going on at the front line.'
>   ■ 'Haig did not care about the loss of life.'
>   ■ 'Haig genuinely believed that the attack was going well.'
>   Explain your answer.
> 4. Compare Source 9 with Source 6 on page 23. Write three sentences commenting on the differences between them.
> 5. From the evidence so far how do you think Haig expected to win the War?

The view from Britain

The courage and bravery of the troops was never in question. Back in Britain stories of individual heroism were spread with great enthusiasm (see Source 10).

Neville's Attack became a celebrated incident and a picture of it was drawn for a London newspaper in 1916 (see Source 4 on page 21). The Germans, however, used this same picture for very different purposes and circulated it with the following caption in ten different languages: 'An English absurdity: football played during storm attack.'

SOURCE 10 From a letter written by a friend of Captain Wilfred Neville of the East Surrey Regiment to Neville's sister, describing his death at the Battle of the Somme

66 *Five minutes before zero time, your brother [Wilfred Neville] strolled up in his usual calm way and we shared a last joke before going over.*

The company went over the top very well, with Soames and your brother kicking off with the company footballs. [While on leave, Neville had bought two footballs for his company to kick across No Man's Land at zero hour!] We had to face very heavy rifle and machine gun fire and nearing the front German trench, the line slackened pace slightly. Seeing this, Wilfred dashed in front with a bomb in his hand and was immediately shot through the head . . . 99

But alongside all the stories of heroism, people in Britain were also receiving daily news of the casualties at the Somme. People were no longer shocked by vast casualty numbers – 20,000 dead were impossible to imagine. But eye-witness reports filtered back to Britain, sometimes in letters such as Source 11 which escaped the army censors. Families came face to face with the horrors of war, maybe for the first time – and face to face with the anger of some of the soldiers having to fight this war.

SOURCE 11 Written by Lieutenant J.A. Raws of the 23rd Battalion in a letter to his family shortly before his death on 23 August 1916

66 *We are lousy, stinking, ragged, unshaven and sleepless. My tunic is rotten with other men's blood and partly spattered with a friend's brains. It is horrible, but why should you people at home not know? The horror was indescribable . . . I want to tell you so that it may be on record, that I honestly believe that Goldie (a mate) and many others were murdered through the stupidity of those in authority.* 99

FIELD MARSHAL HAIG: 'THE BUTCHER OF THE SOMME'?

Politicians, including members of the government, began to wonder whether Haig's approach was working. They accepted that the pressure had been taken off Verdun, but they were concerned about the number of dead and wounded.

Major-General (addressing the men before practising an attack behind the lines). "I WANT YOU TO UNDERSTAND THAT THERE IS A DIFFERENCE BETWEEN A REHEARSAL AND THE REAL THING. THERE ARE THREE ESSENTIAL DIFFERENCES: FIRST, THE ABSENCE OF THE ENEMY. NOW (turning to the Regimental Sergeant-Major) WHAT IS THE SECOND DIFFERENCE?"
Sergeant-Major. "THE ABSENCE OF THE GENERAL, SIR."

SOURCE 14 A cartoon from *Punch* magazine

SOURCE 12 A personal memoir written by Winston Churchill MP in August 1916

> *I view with the utmost pain, this terrible killing of our troops. We have not gained in a month's fighting as much ground as we were expected to gain in the first two hours. We have not advanced two miles in a direct line at any point . . . Nor are we making for any point of military importance; it is all open country which can easily be defended by the use of trenches.*

Activity

It is 1916. You have seen the cartoon in Source 14. Write a letter to the magazine in response to the cartoon. Your letter should either support or complain about the way the generals are fighting the War.

Did Haig make mistakes?

SOURCE 15 Judgements on Haig

SOURCE 13 A letter written to the *Daily Telegraph* by Lord Lansdowne, an ex-Cabinet Minister, on 29 November 1916

> *We are slowly but surely killing off the best of the male population of these islands. Can we afford to go on paying the same sort of price for the same sort of gain?*

This celebrated letter became known as the Lansdowne Letter. It was the first time that a leading politician had openly questioned the way the War was being fought.

1. Source 15 gives some judgements on Haig's leadership. Can you match each sentence up to the character who you think might have said it?

1967 The historian Sir Llewellyn Woodward

1919 Lovat Fraser, a fighting soldier

1922 Colonel J.H. Boraston. He was Haig's personal secretary during the War

1968 Field Marshal Montgomery, who was one of Britain's army chiefs in World War II

It may seem to you that Haig was silly, ignorant or uncaring. The costly tactics used at the Somme were used again and again until the final breakthrough in 1918. But historians have to try to look at things from the perspective of people at the time. For example, Source 17 was written by Haig himself, to explain his tactics, while Source 16 was written by a modern historian.

SOURCE 16 From a book called *Field Marshal Haig*, written by the historian Philip Warner in 1991

66 *If the criterion of a successful general is to win wars, Haig must be judged a success. The cost of victory was appalling, but Haig's military methods were in line with the ideas of the time, when attrition was the method all sides used to achieve victory.*

The full horrors of the First World War make it difficult to reach a clear appraisal of Haig. Those who admit he did eventually push the most powerful army in the world off French soil criticise the cost of the way he did it without offering alternative methods. 99

Our High Command had not advanced beyond the tactics of the Stone Age. They could not think of any other form of warfare, except to throw into battle large numbers of men month after month.

The Battle of the Somme was a great triumph for the genius of British leadership.

Haig's method of winning the War was clumsy, expensive in loss of life, and based on a misreading of the facts.

Haig was unimaginative and dull. Nothing can excuse the casualties of the Somme.

SOURCE 17 Haig's own explanations for his tactics, all written just after the War in 1919

66 ■ *In the course of the struggle, losses are bound to be heavy on both sides, for in this the price of victory is paid. There is no way of avoiding this . . . but our total losses in this war have been no larger than were to be expected.*
■ *We attacked whenever possible, because a defensive policy involves the loss of the initiative.*
■ *The object of all war is victory and a defensive attitude can never bring this about.* 99

In fact many historians have suggested ways in which Haig could have changed his tactics at the Battle of the Somme:
■ When he realised the full-frontal attacks were not breaking through, he could have stopped them. The Germans' advance had already been halted.
■ Haig could have attacked without bombardments, which always warned the Germans that an attack was coming and took away the surprise.
■ The British Navy could have been used to bomb the Germans from the west and Haig could have attacked the Germans' west flank close to the coast of Belgium.
■ Instead of vast waves of INFANTRY going over the top, flexible teams of machine gunners could have been used to attack the weak points in the German trench system without mass loss of life.

---

2. Choose one statement from Sources 15 and 17 that you agree with and one that you disagree with. Explain your choice.
3. Why do you think Haig did not choose any of the options above? Sources 16 and 17 may help.
4. Why do you think there is so much disagreement about Haig?

Activity
It is the anniversary of the Battle of the Somme. You have been asked to make a short radio feature to explain:
■ what happened at the Battle of the Somme
■ whether Haig made mistakes or whether he simply did a difficult job in a difficult situation.

Get into groups and make a feature about five minutes long.

Did technology help break the stalemate?

IN 1914 Germany and Britain were the two most advanced industrial nations in the world. Many of the world's top scientists and inventors were British or German.

Since 1900 there had been many new discoveries and inventions which might be very useful in wartime. Aeroplanes and AIRSHIPS had been flown for the first time. Submarines had been launched. Radio communication had been used. Both countries had built bigger, more powerful ships than any known before.

Yet in trench warfare the battle tactics were just the same as they might have been twenty years earlier. Week after week thousands of soldiers were sent 'over the top' in a human wave, trying to beat the enemy by sheer weight of numbers. Horses, dogs and birds were used by the army in France, as well as new inventions like tanks, aircraft and radio. In this section we investigate a number of case studies to see how important both old methods and new inventions were in the War. Was it the new technology which eventually helped to break the stalemate?

Case study 1:

Horses

In almost every war until the First World War, the CAVALRY had been a most important weapon. Field Marshal Haig had used cavalry with great success in the last war Britain had fought, on the wide, open and dry plains of Southern Africa. In 1914 the generals believed cavalry would still be important. At the start of the War each side had a cavalry force of over 100,000 and believed it would be vital for winning battles.

In fact the mud, the barbed wire and the deadly machine gun fire of the Western Front made a cavalry charge impossible. When it was tried the slaughter was awful. For example, in a cavalry attack on 30 March 1918, only four out of 150 horses survived the charge against the German machine guns.

But although the cavalry charge was a thing of the past the horse was not. Horses proved their worth again and again on the Western Front, even though the work they did was never easy.

More than two and a half million horses and mules were treated in veterinary hospitals in France during the War. Nearly two million were cured and returned to duty.

More than eight million horses died on all sides between 1914 and 1918: 484,143 were from Britain, according to official figures.

SOURCE 1 A horse and water cart stuck in mud at Ypres, August 1917

SOURCE 2 Written by a Royal Artillery officer

The vet insisted Sailor was too old, too thin and unfit for service. He didn't know. He only judged by appearances. Sailor wasn't much to look at, but was worth six horses in the battery [gun team]. If a gun team jibbed [got stuck], we hitched up old Sailor and he pulled them through. If a vehicle got stuck in a ditch, or was too heavy to start, old Sailor moved it. He would work for 24 hours without winking. He was quiet as a lamb and as clever as a thoroughbred, but he looked like nothing on earth, so we lost him. The whole battery kissed him goodbye and the drivers and gunners who fed him nearly cried.

SOURCE 3 From an account by Private Sydney Smith in 1917

I had the terrible experience to witness three horses and six men disappear completely under the mud. It was a sight that will live for ever in my memory; the cries of the trapped soldiers were indescribable as they struggled to free themselves. The last horse went to a muddy grave, keeping his nostrils above the slush until the last second. A spurt of mud told me it was all over.

1. Look at Sources 1 and 2. Why do you think they used horses for these jobs?
2. Do you consider the deaths of millions of horses to be acceptable?

Case study 2:

Dogs and pigeons

Communication between the front line and the headquarters was a real problem in the Great War. Artillery BATTERIES were often positioned a mile behind the front line, and the generals were many more miles behind them. Communication between the artillery and the front line was essential: otherwise, the guns could easily end up pounding their own front lines.

Various methods were used to get messages through. But they all had drawbacks. Telegraph wires could be broken by SHELL fire. Radio messages were very unreliable and could be intercepted at the front line by the enemy, who were only a few hundred yards away. Human messages – even taken by bicycle – were too slow. Motor transport was often unusable where roads had been churned up into rubble and mud by constant shelling followed by rain. What was the solution?

SOURCE 5 A messenger dog with burns on his paws caused by a poison gas attack in 1918

> **SOURCE 4** Colonel Edwin Richardson, a retired army officer, trained dogs for war service at a training school in Scotland. This is an army report about two of his dogs, Airedale terriers called Wolf and Prince
>
> " *During the operations against the Germans, two messenger dogs belonging to this brigade were sent forward at 1.00 a.m. They were attached to front-line officers.*
>
> *After the artillery attack had finished, they were sent back, one at 10.45 a.m. and the other at 12.45 p.m. Both dogs reached Brigade HQ, travelling a distance as the crow flies of 4000 yards over ground they had never seen before and over very difficult land. The dog which left at 12.45 p.m. reached his destination in under the hour, bringing in an important message. This was the first message received, all other communication having failed.* "

Pigeons were also used for sending messages. They turned out to be more reliable than field telegraphs, radios or despatch riders on bicycles. They were always sent in pairs – two males or two females – and could fly distances of up to 60 miles. Their success rate was high: 100,000 pigeons were used in the War and 95 per cent got through with their messages.

SOURCE 6 A poster displayed in Leeds in 1915

1. Why do you think dogs and pigeons were better at carrying messages than humans or technology?
2. Can you think of any big problems with using horses, dogs or pigeons on the Western Front?

Case study 3:

Gas

At half-past five in the afternoon on 22 April 1915 the Germans released about 150 tons of chlorine gas into the air above their trenches at Ypres. They allowed the gas to drift on the wind onto the British trenches about 200 metres away. The troops began to cough and retch and panic set in. This was the first gas attack of the First World War. It struck terror into the troops and from then on gas attacks were a fact of life in the trenches for the soldiers of both sides.

To start with the aim of the attacks was to knock out the enemy soldiers so that your own could attack them more easily. But gradually more and more lethal gases were developed, which killed, blinded, maimed or blistered the enemy.

German, British and French scientists worked on new substances to attack the enemy and tried to perfect new gas masks to protect their own soldiers.

There were two ways of launching a gas attack. You could release the gas and let it be blown onto your enemy by the wind. Or you could pack it into SHELLS and fire them at the enemy trenches. In any case, launching a gas attack was a very dangerous job. If the wind changed direction the gas could blow back into your own trench. Leaks from cylinders were common. And if a gas attack was followed up by your own troops attacking the enemy lines, they needed to be well protected with gas masks, which restricted their mobility and their vision and made breathing difficult.

SOURCE 7 British machine gunners wearing gas masks, 1916

SOURCE 8 Statistics about gas attacks during the War

> British: 178,500 hurt   7,500 killed
> French: 107,250 hurt   22,750 killed
> Germans: 101,650 hurt   5,350 killed
>   Mustard gas, chlorine and phosgene made up 20% of all the shells fired during the War. They caused 15% of all casualties (hurt and killed) but only 1.4% of total deaths.

SOURCE 9 Written by Captain A.F.P. Christison of the Cameron Highlanders

> **Friday 13 July 1917**
> It proved to be a bad day. C Company under Captain Harry Rowan was on my right and at about 0800 hours, the Germans started shelling steadily. One shell landed in my trench almost beside me and did not burst. I felt a burning sensation just above my right knee and heard the man next to me retch and cough . . . I shouted 'Gas' and quickly put on my respirator. The gas alarm immediately sounded and as we were good at our gas drill, only five or six of my company were gassed.
>   Captain Rowan and his men had put on respirators, but after wearing them for some time in the heat of the morning and no attack developing, they thought the original warning had been false as no gas had been smelt. What they did not know was that this was mustard gas, had no smell and had delayed action. The C Company trenches were saturated with the stuff . . . By nightfall, every officer and man was either dead or in hospital.

1. Gas attacks are forbidden in modern warfare by the Geneva Protocol of 1925. Why do you think this is?
2. Do you think it is a sensible rule? Explain your answer.

Case study 4:

Tanks

The most pressing problem if the STALEMATE was to be broken was how to overcome the enemy's machine guns. It was the machine guns which more than anything were responsible for the stalemate. They were so effective that they could cut down whole companies of men in seconds. What was needed was a method of attack that did not expose men to machine gun fire.

In October 1914 a proposal was presented to the British government. It sketched what mechanised warfare would be like. Armoured machines on caterpillar tracks would be brought into position at night. They would advance on the enemy, smashing obstructions on the way and protected from enemy machine guns by their armour. They would sweep enemy trenches with machine gun fire. Behind them, foot-soldiers would advance in short rushes. The proposal said that surprise would be vital. Smoke screens might be used, so that the advance of the armoured vehicles would be hidden from the enemy.

The army rejected the plan. But one wartime minister, Winston Churchill, thought the idea could work. His navy department put money into the idea. After two years of trialling and designing, the first working armoured vehicles were ready. They were carried over on a ship to France on a cool summer's night in 1916. To disguise their invention from the German spies the British covered the armoured vehicles and labelled them 'Water tanks'. The name stuck. From then on armoured vehicles were known as tanks.

SOURCE 10 A photograph taken on 15 September 1916 at the village of Flers on the Somme. This was the first tank to be used in action

SOURCE 11 A description of the inside of a tank from a school textbook, *Britain at War* by Craig Mair, published in 1982

> *The tanks carried a crew of about eight men. Conditions inside were terrible. The engine gave off strong fumes. It became so hot that the crew men wore leather jerkins to protect them when they were thrown against the hot moving parts as the tank lurched across the battlefield. The temperature inside could reach over 38 degrees Centigrade. The cramped and sweaty crew were quickly exhausted. The noise inside was so loud that the commander had to give orders by hand signals.*

1. Look at Source 10. What seems to be the response to this tank?
2. Look at Sources 10 and 11. What is basically wrong with this design?

Tanks in action

Tanks were first used by Field Marshal Haig at the Battle of the Somme. It was a desparate attempt to gain something from the battle when the INFANTRY was being slaughtered. The Germans were amazed. But there were not enough tanks to have a big effect, they were unreliable, and they only travelled at six miles per hour in any case. Worst of all, the great secret weapon was no longer a secret. From then on German positions were defended by anti-tank ditches.

SOURCE 12 By a German war correspondent, 1916

> *When the German lookouts crept out of their dugouts in the mist of the morning and stretched their necks to look for the English, their blood chilled! Mysterious monsters were crawling towards them over the craters . . . The monsters approached slowly, hobbling, rolling and rocking. Nothing stopped them . . . Someone in the trenches said 'The devil is coming', and the word was passed along the line. Tongues of flame leapt from the sides of the iron caterpillars . . . The English infantry came in waves behind.*

SOURCE 13 Written by a British officer, Captain Lionel Ferguson, in 1917

An enemy machine gun opened up on our right . . . and the old tank went right for it, firing a round of shot as it advanced. We stopped to watch the scrap . . . for all the world like a big dog going for a rat.

The machine gun was firing the other way and before the Boche [German] gunners had time to escape, the huge monster was upon them, finishing them for ever.

It was the first blood we had seen that morning and for us spectators, a most thrilling moment.

---

1. Sources 12 and 13 clearly show that the tank could work. Why then did it not break the stalemate on the Western Front in 1917? Source 14 might help you.
2. Who or what do you think Source 15 is aimed at?

SOURCE 14 A description of the Battle of Cambrai in 1917 from a school textbook, *Britain at War* by Craig Mair

The ground here was firm and not churned up by shell fire. At 6.20 a.m. on 20 November 1917, 378 tanks lumbered forward, looking like giant toads. Many carried rolls of brushwood which were thrown down into the anti-tank ditches. They easily crushed the barbed wire and smashed through the German trenches. By four o'clock they had punched a hole ten kilometres wide and six kilometres deep through the German lines. It was a great moment.

Unfortunately now everything started to go wrong. There were not enough infantry to take advantage of this huge hole. The Germans soon began to recover and fight back. By evening over 100 tanks had run out of petrol or had broken down. Sixty-five had been destroyed by enemy gunfire. All those tanks were now stranded in enemy territory. The surviving crews were exhausted and they could do nothing as the cavalry, sent in to take advantage of the breakthrough, were cut to pieces by a few machine guns. In the following days the British infantry were gradually pushed back again and the War returned to its normal course of slaughter.

THE TANK is a travelling fortress that clears the way for our soldiers.

It cuts through the wire under fire
It saves lives
It is our War discovery
It is a matter of pride to help to build Tanks.

SOURCE 15 A government poster of 1917

Case study 5:

Aircraft

The aeroplane was a relatively new invention. Britain was the only country to enter the First World War with a properly trained airforce. Yet at the start of the War no one was quite sure how useful the aeroplane would be.

Flying was risky. In 1914 planes were still very basic. They were nicknamed 'string bags'. They were built with just wire, wooden struts and canvas, around a very basic engine. All sorts of things could go wrong, and often did. A plane had no guns, no navigation instruments, no radio and no parachute, and the pilots needed to use sign language to talk to each other. However, the planes quickly showed how useful they were in RECONNAISSANCE. In mid-September 1914 the Germans were on the verge of a breakthrough to Paris which could have won them the War. British aerial photographs showed a gap in the German lines which allowed British troops to advance, forcing the Germans to withdraw.

---

1. Look at Source 16. Is there anything in the photograph that might be of use to the British commanders on the Western Front?

SOURCE 16 This aerial photograph was taken on 19 July 1915 during preparations for the Battle of Loos in Belgium

As each side's aircraft began to provide useful information about the enemy, it became important to stop them. So fighter planes were developed to attack them and shoot them down. The only method of defence against another aircraft was counter-attack. The 'dogfights' that took place captured the imagination of the public. The air aces (five confirmed kills made you an ace) became heroes. German fighter pilots included the famous 'Red Baron' of Germany, Baron Manfred von Richthofen, who shot down 80 enemy planes. British pilots included Captain Albert Ball, who shot down 43 enemy planes before he was killed at the age of only twenty. The successes of air aces provided a welcome change from reports of mass slaughter on the WESTERN FRONT.

SOURCE 17 *The Last Flight of Captain Ball – 17 May 1917*, a painting by Norman Arnold

During the War aircraft technology improved greatly. New designs were introduced. New fighting tactics were developed. By 1918 aircraft could carry machine guns, bombs and cameras, and could fly hundreds of kilometres on a single tank of fuel.

SOURCE 18 An account by Lieutenant Ralph Silk, written in 1978. He was an observer in a Reconnaissance Squadron. The event took place at the very end of the War, on 24 October 1918

> I had already made two flights over the enemy's lines that day, bombing, strafing [machine gunning] and taking photographs. I had retired to my tent for rest when the Squadron Commander lifted the tent flap and said, 'Silk, you will have to go up again. The Huns [Germans] are withdrawing their guns on the Le Cateau road. I want you to blast the lot' . . . I shook hands with him and rushed off to the waiting machine.
>
> Over the lines, a number of enemy Fokker machines swooped out of the sun upon our four RE8 machines, the air was full of wings and bullets; when my machine gave a lurch, I turned my head to my pilot, he had slumped over the controls, mortally wounded. Next, I had a gunshot wound in the head. The machine went into a spin and finally crashed upon some trees near Le Cateau. I can faintly remember being lowered to the ground, then passed out . . .

2. Pilots became 'aces'; 'aces' became heroes and celebrities. Use the evidence in this section to explain in your own words how this happened.
3. Look back at the information on aircraft reconnaissance on page 48, then compare it to Source 18. How did the work and equipment of a reconnaissance squadron change between 1914 and 1918?

1. Divide your page in half. Head one column 'Strengths' and the other column 'Weaknesses'. Then fill it in for each of the following: horses, dogs and birds, gas, tanks, aircraft.
2. Which do you think was the most important technological development during the War?
3. Did any of these developments help break the stalemate? Support your answer using the evidence on pages 44–49.

THE Great War was the first war to have a major impact on the lives of ordinary people back in Britain. In some ways everyone in Britain was 'fighting the War' and everyone's life was changed by it.

Hating the Germans

The first job of the government was to make sure that people in Britain stayed in favour of the War. One way of doing this was to whip up people's hatred of the Germans, so the government produced anti-German PROPAGANDA. Some of it was true. Much of it was not.

In 1915 the government published a report on German atrocities in Belgium during the first months of the War. The report quoted hundreds of 'eye-witness' reports of German cruelty. One person said he'd seen a soldier drive his BAYONET into a child's stomach, lift the child into the air on his bayonet, and carry it away while he and his comrades were singing. Another report told of a twelve-year-old boy whose hands had been cut off by the Germans because he clung to his parents who were being thrown on a fire.

Early in 1915 one of the most famous propaganda stories of all began to circulate – that there was a German factory where human corpses gathered from the battlefield were melted down so that the fat could be made into soap. In fact, captions to two separate photographs of dead horses and dead men had been swapped around.

SOURCE 1 From an advertisement for Black Cat cigarettes

SOURCE 2 From the magazine *John Bull*

> *If by chance you should discover one day in a restaurant that you are being served by a German waiter, you will throw the soup in his foul face.*

The government's campaign of hatred against the Germans was very successful. German people living in Britain were attacked. In 1915 the government decided to hold prisoner all Germans between the ages of seventeen and 45. German old men, women and children were sent back to Germany.

By 1917 anti-German feeling was so strong that even the King decided that he had to change his family name from Saxe-Coburg-Gotha to Windsor!

Civilian casualties

In the early months of the War people feared that Britain would be invaded. On 17 December 1914 the British people read these headlines in their morning newspapers.

GERMANS CREEP OUT TO ATTACK EAST COAST . . . SCARBOROUGH, HARTLEPOOL AND WHITBY SHELLED FOR 30 MINUTES

In fact, 119 people, including babies and children, had been killed. Source 3 shows how this German attack was used as propaganda by the government.

50,000,000 CARTOONS WINNING THE WAR
Black Cat Cigarettes

Death drinks the toast of *Blood* — of slain soldiers and civilians, and of innocent women and children, killed wherever the German troops have over-run.

This grim picture shows the inevitable fate the Kaiser has prepared for himself and Germany. War and Hunger are leading him by the hand — *to the end*.

The *biting truth* of these extraordinary cartoons — there are 140 different ones in colour — completely and finally proves WHY we are at war with Germany. And that is why every packet of BLACK CAT cigarettes (4d., 3½d., or 3d.) contains one of the *50,000,000* of these cartoons, fifty million *truths* to combat German *lies*.

SOURCE 3 A poster issued by the government soon after the attack on Scarborough

SOURCE 5 The scene after the Silvertown Disaster, 1917

1. Why do you think the Germans bombed the east coast towns?
2. How might it have helped their war effort?
3. How do you think the inhabitants responded to this attack?

In 1915 the Germans started to send great AIRSHIPS called Zeppelins on bombing raids to Britain. These were 650 feet long and could drop up to 27 tons of bombs. East Anglia, London and towns in the South East were the main targets. Hundreds of people were killed.

SOURCE 4 An eye-witness account of a Zeppelin Raid in 1915

The whole street seemed to explode. There was smoke and flames all over, but the worst of it was the screams of the dying and the wounded and mothers looking frantically for their kids.

Another serious incident took place on 19 January 1917 at Silvertown in East London. A MUNITIONS factory went up in flames and exploded, killing 69 people and injuring 400. Factories and nearby houses were blown to bits.

SOURCE 6 An eye-witness account by Mabel Bastable, who was a schoolgirl in 1917

There were shouts of 'Fire!', well, you couldn't miss it, the whole place was lit up. We were all outside looking . . .
I went upstairs to get a shawl. Suddenly, I was downstairs and the house was on top of me. It's funny but I can't really remember hearing the explosion . . . Our house was blown down right enough.
We had to walk a long way to find somewhere to put up [sleep], my Mum's sister I think we stayed with. We didn't go up to Silvertown again . . . I didn't go to school again. There was no school, no house, so there was no point.

A total of 1500 British CIVILIANS were killed during the War. That might seem low to us by the standards of more recent wars, but at that time it was very high compared to previous wars.

Activity

Write a propaganda report on the explosion at Silvertown using the evidence in Sources 5 and 6. You should slant your report to whip up hatred of the German enemy. Remember that this is the result of an accident and not of bombing, but if you are clever you can still use it as propaganda.

DORA

People's lives were also greatly affected by the passing of the Defence of the Realm Act, or DORA. This listed all the things people were no longer allowed to do now that Britain was at war, and also gave the government special powers. The first measures were introduced on 8 August 1914. During the War other rules were added.

Under DORA the people of Britain were not allowed to:

- talk about naval or military matters in public places
- spread rumours about military affairs
- trespass on railways or bridges
- fly a kite
- light bonfires or fireworks
- buy binoculars
- trespass on allotments
- melt down gold or silver
- give bread to dogs, chickens or horses
- use invisible ink when writing abroad
- buy whisky or brandy in a railway refreshment room or similar place
- ring church bells.

The government of Britain could:

- try any civilian breaking these laws
- take possession of any factory or workshop
- take any land it needed
- CENSOR newspapers.

As the War continued, the government brought in many other measures. For example:

- it introduced British Summer Time (putting the clocks forward an hour) to give more daylight for work in the evening
- it cut down on pub opening hours
- it gave instructions for beer to be watered down
- customers in pubs were not allowed to buy rounds of drinks.

---

1. Write the heading DORA in your book and then make two lists – one headed 'Sensible Ideas' and the other 'Stupid Ideas'. Put each of the measures described above into one of the lists.
2. Can you think of reasons for any of the laws in your second list?
3. Which of these measures do you think would be popular and which would be unpopular?

Feeding the realm

One of the aims of DORA was to prevent food shortages. At first, food shortage problems were caused by the British people themselves. As soon as war broke out they panicked and bought large amounts of food which they hoarded at home. Shops sold out completely within a few days. However, everybody gradually calmed down and shortages did not really become serious until the end of 1916.

Until that time much of Britain's food was still imported. But by 1917 the Germans were using their submarines to stop supply ships from getting through. In April 1917 Britain had only six weeks' worth of wheat stores! Food prices rose sharply and queues for food grew. It was a bleak year for most people. Coal was so short that in October it was RATIONED according to the number of rooms in the house.

In 1917 it was clear that the DORA measures were not enough to reduce the amount of food being eaten or increase the amount being produced. The government tried to operate a voluntary ration scheme. It asked people to limit themselves to four pounds of bread, two and a half pounds of meat and three quarters of a pound of sugar each week. The King and Queen limited themselves to this ration and if you followed their example you were issued with a blue ribbon!

But the campaign failed – shortages of bread and potatoes continued. Many working people could not afford to buy meat and sugar anyway – their diet had consisted mainly of bread even before the rationing was introduced! The rich, on the other hand, continued to live as luxuriously as ever. Food was available for those who could afford it – on the BLACK MARKET if necessary.

Desperate attempts were made to grow more food. Nearly everybody started to keep an allotment where they could grow food. They turned parks and tennis courts into vegetable plots where they grew potatoes, turnips and carrots and kept chickens.

Under DORA the government had powers to take over land for growing food. In 1917 it decided to plough up an extra two and a half million acres of land. The amount of land used for farming increased from eleven million acres in 1914 to fourteen million in 1918. However, many farm workers had joined the army, and so much of the work on this extra land was carried out by the new Women's Land Army. Prisoners of war and conscientious objectors (men who refused to join the army: see page 56) were used as well.

SOURCE 7 A 'Land Girl' painted by Cecil Aldin

When women were asked to sign up for the Women's Land Army 30,000 responded immediately. They did work that would have been done mainly by men before the War, and were paid the same wages as men. The work was hard – stone-picking, weeding, pulling turnips and haymaking. It made sense for the women to dress like men, but this made many people uneasy. As Source 8 shows, the government was keen for the women still to behave as people at the time thought women should.

SOURCE 9 Evidence of food shortages

SOURCE 8 Instructions to the members of the Women's Land Army

You are doing a man's work and so you are dressed rather like a man; but remember that . . . because you wear a smock and trousers you should take care to behave like an English girl who expects chivalry and respect from every one she meets. Noisy or ugly behaviour brings discredit, not only on yourself but upon the uniform, and the whole Women's Land Army. When people see you pass show them that an English girl who is working for her Country on the land is the best sort of girl.

Despite all these measures, by 1918 the situation was getting worse for most people. Food queues grew even longer. Signs of malnutrition were beginning to appear among the poorest people. The rich, on the other hand, still had plenty to eat. Resentment of the rich was growing fast. So to share the food round more fairly the government introduced compulsory rationing. Sugar was rationed from January 1918, and from April so were meat, butter, cheese and margarine. Everybody was issued with a ration card, and registered with a local butcher and grocer. Each person could have fifteen ounces of meat, five ounces of bacon and four ounces of butter or margarine per week.

Rationing worked. Queueing for food soon became a thing of the past. And historians agree that by the time rationing ended the health of the poorest people in Britain was actually better than it had been in peacetime – partly because rationing meant they got a better share of healthy food.

SOURCE 10 From a government leaflet published during the War. A crust of bread is speaking

I am a slice of bread. I am wasted once a day by 48,000,000 people of Britain. I am 'the bit left over'; the slice eaten absent-mindedly when really I wasn't needed. I am the waste crust.

If you collected me and my companions for a whole week you would find that we amounted to 9380 tons of good bread.

WASTED! Nine shiploads of good bread!
SAVE ME, AND I WILL SAVE YOU!

1. Look back at the list of 'stupid ideas' you made for question 1 on page 52. Does the evidence on the rest of this page help you to explain why these ideas were introduced?
2. Draw a timeline for the period August 1914 to April 1918. Mark on it the different methods used to feed Britain. Which one of these measures was the most important?

How did the factories keep going?

When war broke out industries such as textiles and dressmaking, which employed a lot of women, suffered because people no longer wanted to buy so many clothes. Many women lost their jobs. However, as more and more men went off to fight, somebody had to replace them in the factories and on the farms. Gradually, women began to take on men's jobs. But this did not happen overnight.

In 1915 the government was faced with a serious shortage of SHELLS and bullets. Many more workers were needed, but of course the men were joining the army. Instead, the government would have to recruit as many women to work in factories as possible. A march to publicise the campaign to recruit women was organised by David Lloyd George, who was minister in charge of MUNITIONS, and Mrs Pankhurst, the SUFFRAGETTE leader. This was the first time the government had accepted that women could play a vital role in winning the War.

The government drew up a register of women who were available for work. Over 100,000 registered, but only 5000 of them were given jobs, mainly because employers and male workers were prejudiced against having women working in industry.

The trade unions as well were very suspicious of women coming into factories and doing men's jobs. They were worried that women would work for lower wages and so the men would lose their jobs for good. However, in 1915 the government and the unions came to an agreement. Women workers were to be paid the same as men, but women would only be allowed to take over men's jobs 'for the duration of the War, or till sufficient male labour should again be available'.

Later in 1915 the army was so short of munitions that the government set up its own munitions factories, where there were no male employers or workers to stop women being employed.

> **1.** Was the campaign to recruit women workers successful? Explain your answer.

A turning point came when CONSCRIPTION was introduced in 1916. At this point many factory owners finally realised that they needed to take on women to replace the male workers who had joined the army.

Before the War it had been assumed that women could only do light, indoor work which did not need much strength or skill. This was why so many women worked as domestic servants. These views were soon shown to be wrong. During the War women learned new skills within a much shorter time than the normal training period. In many jobs women performed better than the men they were replacing, even though the conditions they worked in were often tougher than they had been for men before the War.

SOURCE 12 A munitions factory painted by E.F. Skinner

SOURCE 13 A fitter at the London Bus Company in 1918

SOURCE 11 A government report written after the War describing the situation in 1915

> *In every industrial district without exception, there was opposition to the introduction of women. In some cases this opposition led to strikes, in other cases it took the form of refusal to work with or train women, or attempts to discredit their efforts.*

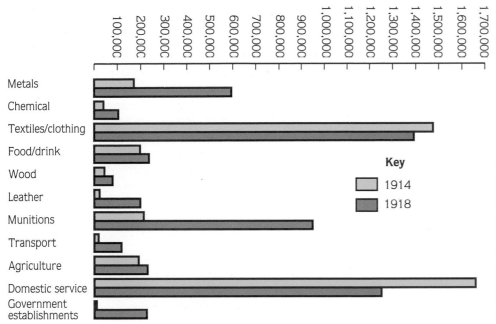

	100,000	200,000	300,000	400,000	500,000	600,000	700,000	800,000	900,000	1,000,000	1,100,000	1,200,000	1,300,000	1,400,000	1,500,000	1,600,000	1,700,000	

Metals
Chemical
Textiles/clothing
Food/drink
Wood
Leather
Munitions
Transport
Agriculture
Domestic service
Government establishments

Key
1914
1918

◀ **SOURCE 16** Women employed in industry in 1914 and 1918. These figures come mainly from the Report of the War Cabinet Committee on Women in Industry, 1919. The figures for domestic service, agriculture and transport are author's estimates

2. Look at the figures in Source 16 carefully. Find two industries where the number of women workers actually went down during the War. Why was this?
3. Some of the biggest increases were in metal industries, government establishments and agriculture. Why was this?
4. ■ 'The War didn't lead to more women going out to work, but it changed the types of jobs women did.'
   Say whether you agree or disagree with this statement and why.
5. Do you think that by 1918 most men had accepted women as being equal to them?

SOURCE 14 Women workers at a Lancashire colliery in September 1918. The total workforce at this colliery was 9000, of whom 500 were women. They did not work underground, but did surface work such as sorting or carrying coal

You have seen the ways in which people's lives were completely changed by the War. Working in pairs discuss the following questions:
1. Which of these changes do you think made British society better and fairer?
2. Which changes took their freedom away from people?
3. Which changes would you have kept once the War had ended?
4. Which changes do you think were actually kept after the War had ended?

SOURCE 15 Tar sprayers resurfacing a road in London

Did anyone object to the War?

WHEN Britain declared war on Germany in 1914, the vast majority of British people supported the War. The government put out lots of PROPAGANDA to make sure people continued to support it. The newspapers – which were the main source of information for most people – were in favour of the War in any case. The Defence of the Realm Act made it difficult for people to criticise the way the War was being fought without getting into trouble. Only a few people publicly criticised the War. However, as the War progressed this situation began to change.

The conchies

From 1914 until 1916 the government relied on volunteers to fight in the army. But the huge numbers of casualties in France meant the government needed more and more soldiers. By 1916 it was clear that volunteers were not enough.

Many people in Britain were also angry to see some young men still enjoying themselves at home while others were risking their lives for their country. Pressure grew on the government to force all men to join up and fight. So in January 1916 the government brought in the Military Service Act, which introduced CONSCRIPTION for all single men between the ages of eighteen and 41. A second Act was passed in March 1916 to include married men.

Men who wanted to be exempt (excused) from military service had to appear before a military tribunal to present their case for being excused. The military tribunal included people from the army and a 'jury' made up of local people. Conscripts could be exempted if:
■ they proved they were not physically fit to serve *or*
■ they proved their job was essential to the war effort *or*
■ they proved they had genuine reasons of conscience for not wanting to fight. These men were known as 'conscientious objectors' or 'conchies'.

If the military tribunal thought their reasons were good enough they could get a Certificate of Exemption.

Roughly 16,000 men refused to join the army because they were conscientious objectors. Some of them believed that war itself was wrong and did not want to support it in any way. Others did not want to kill fellow human beings, but would help the War in other ways.

Here are some case studies gathered by the No-Conscription Fellowship, which supported conchies. They were published in 1919.

Case study 1: Stephen Hobhouse

Stephen Hobhouse is 36, married and a Quaker [Quakers believe in complete non-violence].

Despite his wealthy background, he has spent much of his adult life doing social work among the poor of the East End of London. He has for many years been opposed to war and military service because of deeply held religious views.

There can be no doubt as to his courage and to his willingness to face any danger or trouble for the sake of his religion. He spent some time in Turkey working with the poor and homeless.

He is undoubtedly physically unfit for active service and would be useless to the army. He has heart and stomach trouble and is extremely short-sighted.

His three brothers are in the army and his family are strongly in favour of the War, but they believe that he should be allowed to continue his work in the service of his God and his country.

He is now serving a sentence of two years. He has already served one sentence of 112 days' hard labour.

He says 'Four months in a prison cell have only confirmed my belief that war and violence are not the ways to overcome evil . . .'

Case study 2: G.H. Stuart Beavis

Beavis was 34 when the War broke out. He has lived in Germany and France and speaks both languages. He was a teacher of languages at a Working Men's College in London.

It was his great belief in the brotherhood of all nations which caused him to refuse conscription. In May 1916 he was taken to France. He was told that he was now in the war zone and liable to be shot for refusing to obey orders. He was tried and sentenced to death! This was later changed to ten years in prison.

Case study 3: Clifford Allen

Clifford Allen was 25 in 1914. He was well educated and had become a journalist. He was one of the founders of the No-Conscription Fellowship in November 1914 and was its first chairman. From 1916 onwards, he received a string of prison sentences with hard labour for refusing to join up. He gave the following reasons at his trial:

'I believe that you sitting here and the people of all nations on both sides want peace. I believe that it is the fault of the governments that this has not happened. I will not take part in any war which I believe could be stopped immediately. I resist war because I love freedom. Conscription is the denial of freedom. You can shut me up in prison over and over again, but you cannot imprison my free spirit.'

1. Stephen Hobhouse could have been excused from military service on grounds of ill health or because he was doing work 'of national importance', yet he chose not to. Why do you think this was?
2. Why did Stuart Beavis object to the War?

Activity

Clifford Allen is critical of governments. He thinks the War could be stopped right away. He believes that war itself is wrong. He is opposed to conscription because it takes away the freedom of individuals. He is prepared to go to prison for his beliefs.

In pairs, act out a conversation between Clifford Allen and a member of a military tribunal who is trying to convince him that he should play an active part in the War.

SOURCE 1 This cartoon was published in a pacifist newspaper called the *Workers' Dreadnought* in 1916

What did people think of the conchies?

As you can imagine, a lot of pressure was put on the conchies. They were given some support by certain magazines (see Source 1) and by organisations such as the No-Conscription Fellowship, a group of conscientious objectors. But they were treated as if they were cowards, traitors or criminals by the army, by the government, and even by many ordinary people in Britain. White feathers (a symbol of cowardice) were handed out to young men who had not joined the army, regardless of any reasons they might have had for not fighting.

Even those who agreed to do war work other than fighting were outcasts. The government found it impossible to get employers to take on conchies in their factories. It ended up setting up its own work camps where conchies had to do work such as quarrying and crushing stone or repairing roads.

1. Write a sentence summarising the message of each of the cartoons in Sources 1 and 2.
2. Which side would you take?

SOURCE 2 This cartoon was published in *John Bull* magazine, May 1918. The caption read 'This little pig stayed at home'

DID ANYONE OBJECT TO THE WAR?

Sources 3–5 show the range of attitudes at the time.

> **SOURCE 3** Comments made by members of military tribunals to conchies
>
> ■ *It is such people as you who cause wars . . .*
> ■ *You are only fit to be on the end of a German bayonet . . .*
> ■ *You are nothing but a shivering mass of unwholesome fat . . .*
> ■ *A man who would not help to defend his own country is a coward . . .*

> **SOURCE 4** From a speech by the government minister Lord Derby in the House of Lords on 24 May 1917
>
> *They are prepared to let other men in this country fight for their freedom, but they will not even assist their country by doing any work at all for the nation.*

> **SOURCE 5** From a report by a Quaker conchy, quoted in *The Modern World* by Tim Wood and Chris Jordan, published in 1989
>
> *It was right at the beginning that I learnt that the only people from whom I could expect sympathy were soldiers and not the civilians.*
>
> *I was waiting in the guardroom when five soldiers under arrest came in. When they asked me what I was in for, I was as simple as possible. 'I am a Quaker and I refused to join the army because I think that war is murder.'*
>
> *'Murder,' one of them whispered. 'It's bloody murder.'*
>
> *As they went away they each came up to me and shook me by the hand – 'Stick to it matey,' they said, one after the other.*

1. What do you think the speaker meant by the first comment in Source 3?
2. Which of the sources above suggest that the conchies were cowards and traitors?
3. Do you think these were fair comments?

What happened to the conchies?

Most conchies joined up to do war work in the medical services or support services. For example, they became stretcher bearers and played as brave a part as anyone in the fight against the Germans on the WESTERN FRONT.

Only about 1500 conchies refused every kind of alternative service. They went to prison until the end of the War. Ten died in prison, another 63 died soon after release, and 31 of them went mad as a result of their experiences.

> **SOURCE 6** An account of the treatment of conscientious objectors in a military prison in England, written in 1928
>
> *At Cleethorpes, a War Resister called James Brightmore was put in a pit three feet by two feet and twelve feet deep with two feet of water in the bottom. He was kept there for four days. He was told by an officer that five of his companions had been sent to France and shot, and that he would be the next to go.*
>
> *Another man called Jack Gray was put into a sack, thrown into a pond eight times and pulled out by a rope around his body.*

> **SOURCE 7** While in military prisons in France, several conchies were given severe punishments, including 'crucifixion', which meant being tied to a gun carriage for hours. A description written in 1928
>
> *. . . Our ankles were tied together and our arms then tied tightly at the wrists to the cross and we had to remain in that position for two hours.*
>
> *The second evening we were placed with our faces to the barbed wire of a fence . . . I found myself drawn so closely to the fence that when I wished to turn my head I had to do so very carefully to avoid my face being torn. To make matters worse, it came on to rain and a bitterly cold wind blew across the top of the hill.*

1. Do you think the conscientious objectors were cowards or very brave men? Use Sources 1–7 to support your answer.

One man's experience: Siegfried Sassoon

Most of the people we have studied in this section were not famous. Their opposition to the War was only known to the few people closest to them. There were others, however, whose opposition was more public. We are going to look at the views of one famous person, the poet Siegfried Sassoon, and see how his views changed during the War.

Siegfried Sassoon was born in 1886. He was a writer and a poet. He came from a very comfortable background in the south of England. Apart from writing, he spent much of his time fox-hunting or playing cricket and golf.

He joined the army in July 1914, before war broke out. He fought bravely on the Western Front, won the Military Cross (a medal for bravery) for a single-handed attack on a trench, and was recommended for a Victoria Cross. He was wounded in 1916 during the Battle of the Somme. Back home in Britain his war poetry quickly made him famous (see Source 6 on page 36).

Sassoon's poems contained many attacks on people who were not directly involved in the fighting yet who supported the War – the old men, the generals, the journalists, the civilians (see Source 9).

Sassoon returned to France to fight, but he became totally opposed to the War. He was not a conchy, but he hated the War because he thought it was unnecessary. He also hated the attitude of the people at home, because he thought they had no idea what life in the trenches was really like.

But he still continued to fight. In July 1917 he was wounded again.

Back in England, encouraged by friends who were against the War, he made the statement in Source 10 to his commanding officer.

> **SOURCE 8** Written by Sassoon years after the War about his decision to join the army in July 1914
>
> *I rushed to the conclusion that war was a certainty, so what else could I do but try to have a gun in my hands when the Germans arrived, even if I did not know how to fire it properly? . . . I said to myself that I was ready to meet whatever the War might ask of me. After all, dying for one's native land was believed to be the most glorious thing one could possibly do.*

> **SOURCE 9** *The General*, a poem written in 1917
>
> *'Good morning; good morning!' the general said*
> *When we met him last week on our way to the line.*
> *Now the soldiers he smiled at are most of 'em dead.*
> *And we're cursing his staff for incompetent swine.*
> *'He's a cheery old card,' grunted Harry to Jack*
> *As they slogged up to Arras with rifle and pack.*
> *But he did for them both with his plan of attack.*

> **SOURCE 10** Sassoon's statement
>
> *A Soldier's Declaration*
> *I believe the War is being prolonged by those who have the power to end it. I believe that this war upon which I entered as a war of defence and liberation has now become a war of conquest and aggression. I have seen and endured the sufferings of the troops and I can no longer be a party to prolong these sufferings for ends which I believe to be evil and unjust.*

The statement was printed in the *Bradford Pioneer* on 27 July 1917. Three days later it was read out in the House of Commons, and the next day it was printed in the *Daily Mail* and *The Times*.

He expected to be COURT MARTIALLED, but instead he was sent for psychiatric treatment in a hospital specialising in victims of shell-shock. In 1918 he returned once again to fight in France, where he was again wounded.

After the War, Sassoon became a PACIFIST. In 1919 he announced, 'I have pledged myself to oppose war in every way I can.'

1. How did Sassoon's view of the War change between 1914 and 1919?
2. Look at Source 8. Why did Sassoon join the army in the first place?
3. Sources 9 and 10 give similar reasons for Sassoon's opposition to the War. What are they?
4. Which of Sources 9 and 10 do you think expresses his views more clearly?

What kind of country did the soldiers come back to?

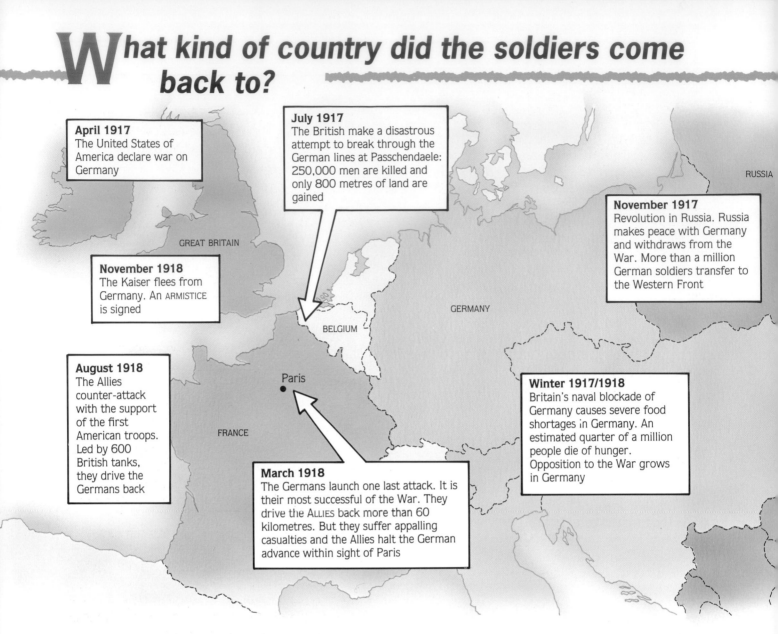

April 1917
The United States of America declare war on Germany

July 1917
The British make a disastrous attempt to break through the German lines at Passchendaele: 250,000 men are killed and only 800 metres of land are gained

November 1917
Revolution in Russia. Russia makes peace with Germany and withdraws from the War. More than a million German soldiers transfer to the Western Front

November 1918
The Kaiser flees from Germany. An ARMISTICE is signed

August 1918
The Allies counter-attack with the support of the first American troops. Led by 600 British tanks, they drive the Germans back

March 1918
The Germans launch one last attack. It is their most successful of the War. They drive the ALLIES back more than 60 kilometres. But they suffer appalling casualties and the Allies halt the German advance within sight of Paris

Winter 1917/1918
Britain's naval blockade of Germany causes severe food shortages in Germany. An estimated quarter of a million people die of hunger. Opposition to the War grows in Germany

RUSSIA
GREAT BRITAIN
BELGIUM
GERMANY
Paris
FRANCE

SOURCE 1 The final stages of the War on the Western Front

1. Draw a timeline to cover the period from April 1917 to November 1918. Mark on it the information given in Source 1.
2. Choose one event from Source 1 that was particularly important in breaking the stalemate on the Western Front. Explain your choice.

Armistice Day

At the eleventh hour of the eleventh day of the eleventh month of 1918 an ARMISTICE was signed. The Germans surrendered. All fighting stopped. The bloodiest war the world had ever known left almost nine million dead, of whom nearly a million were from Britain and its Empire.

'The heroes' return

Only a few weeks later, on 14 December 1918, there was a General Election. The new COALITION government, including Liberal and Conservative MPs, announced that its aims were: 'To make Britain a fit country for heroes to live in' and 'to get back to normal'.

1. Divide a large sheet of paper in half. At the top of each column write one of the aims of the government.
2. Now, working in groups, make a list of some of the measures people in Britain might expect the government to take to achieve each aim.
3. In a class discussion decide which measures a) soldiers returning to Britain, and b) women working in munitions factories might think most important.

YESTERDAY-THE TRENCHES

SOURCE 2
Posters published
by the Labour Party

TO-DAY-UNEMPLOYED

The government had planned to release men from the army slowly, over a number of years, but many soldiers wanted to get home to their families straight away. Over two million men, some of them healthy, some disabled and wounded, returned from the trenches. For many of them the problems started immediately, as you can see in Sources 2–5.

SOURCE 3 Written by the novelist Barbara Cartland in 1978

In the country, chicken farms, wayside cafes and garages have sprung up like mushrooms — all run by ex-servicemen. Many of these have already gone bankrupt and their owners have joined the patient queues of hollow-eyed men . . . waiting for a job.

SOURCE 4 Soldiers being fitted with artificial legs. By 1920 more than 40,000 men were fitted with artificial limbs

SOURCE 5 An account by Grace Hayward, who lived in Ore, a small village near Hastings, during the War

After the dreadful First War, they came up and used to stand outside our gate and sing. They were so poverty struck, those that had gone and fought for us . . .
They'd lost arms, been blinded. They were begging, selling matches. They used to stand about playing an old accordion, standing on one leg. Those poor men.

For the returning heroes there was only limited unemployment benefit, and there was no National Health Service. Housing for many was cramped, unhealthy or non-existent. Many unemployed or wounded soldiers relied on their families or on charity to look after them. Many of the disabled did not qualify for an army pension. To make matters worse, between 1918 and 1920 a terrible flu epidemic hit Britain. Thousands of people died in Britain, and twenty million died around the world – more people than died in the War itself.

The new government passed various reforms between 1918 and 1920:

■ **1918** The Education Act raised the school leaving age to fourteen.

■ **1919** The Ministry of Health Act set up a government department to check living conditions and to introduce measures to fight illness.

■ **1919** The Housing Act ordered local authorities to provide houses for 'the heroes'.

■ **1920** The Unemployment Insurance Act extended the 1911 Act (see page 4) to anyone earning less than £250 a year.

4. What are the people in Source 2 complaining about?
5. What reasons can you find for the fact that some ex-soldiers had to turn to begging to survive?
6. Which of the government's reforms would have been of most use to the soldiers in Sources 2–5?
7. Which of the reforms were brought in as a result of the War?
8. Do you think the government was succeeding in creating a country fit for heroes to live in?

'Homes fit for heroes'

This was the slogan of the government's housing campaign. Even before the War Britain had been short of houses. To make matters worse, during the War many houses had not been well looked after and had become unfit to live in. When millions of soldiers suddenly arrived back in England the problem became severe. Many of them could not rely on relatives or friends to house them or their families.

The Housing Act of 1919 meant that local councils had to provide homes for the working classes in their areas. Over 200,000 new houses were built in the next three years. Even so, this was nowhere near enough for all the soldiers and their families, because the birth rate increased enormously after the War.

While soldiers were waiting for new council houses they had to live in temporary accommodation, some of which was very bad. In Brighton and Hove on the south coast of England, for example, some soldiers and their families were housed in old slums to start with.

1. Look at Source 6. St Helens Council did a good job. But what problem did it not solve?

SOURCE 6 A report from St Helens in Lancashire in the early 1920s

The Council was very good – it built very good houses. The standard was very high. They had some first class supervisory staff. The Clerk of the Works, who had been a builder himself, was on the job all day long. The queues for the houses were miles long. Everyone put their names on the list. They jumped for joy if they got a council house.

SOURCE 7 Lynton Mews, Bermondsey, London, in 1919

2. Study Source 8. Working with a partner make a list of all the ways in which the new home is better than the old one.
3. Are there any ways in which it is worse?

SOURCE 8 An artist's reconstruction of a house in Hereford Street, Brighton. The old house was demolished in 1925 and the new council house was built in its place

New products

Sources 9–13 show adverts for new products which first became available soon after the War. Some of them had been developed or made cheaper as a direct result of the War. These new products changed the lives of people who could afford them, often for the better.

▼**SOURCE 9** An advert for electric lights

OSRAM LAMPS
THE LIGHT FOR ALL
WONDERFUL! 20 HOURS FOR ONE PENNY!

▲**SOURCE 11** An advert for motorcycles

B.S.A MOTOR BICYCLES

XCEL ELECTRIC DOMESTIC APPLIANCES
Wonderland!

▲**SOURCE 12** A 1920s advert for domestic appliances

▼**SOURCE 10** An advert for Austin cars, 1926

The Austin Twelve

NEW REDUCED PRICES............£295 to £425
AUSTIN TWENTY MODELS FROM....£475 to £715
AUSTIN SEVEN.........................£149

Send for full Catalogue.

The AUSTIN MOTOR CO., Ltd., Longbridge, BIRMINGHAM.
LONDON: Showrooms, Service Depot & Hire Dept.: 479–483, OXFORD STREET W.I (near Marble Arch).

For Unoccupied Evenings

Bachelor quarters may be the snuggest in the world, but nowhere else on the long winter evenings is one so often at a loose end.

Install a Marconiphone Wireless Receiver, and you will never be at a loss for entertainment. The British Broadcasting Company take the solution of the problem out of your hands. Their admirably varied programmes are yours whenever you care to "tune in."

The Marconiphone is the Receiver on which you can always rely, for in it is summed up everything for which the name "Marconi" stands in Wireless.

The best Christmas present—for your family or your friends—is

Admirably adapted for general purposes throughout Great Britain, the **MARCONIPHONE V2** is a two-valve receiver of extreme sensitiveness and perfect workmanship. Price complete with head-phones, valves, batteries, etc., including B.B.C. Tariff 15/-,

£19 : 4 : 6

The **Marconiphone**
The Triumph of the Master Mind

MARCONI'S WIRELESS TELEGRAPH CO. LTD., MARCONI HOUSE, STRAND, W.C.2
Principality Buildings, Queen Street, CARDIFF: 104 St. Vincent Street, GLASGOW: 10 Cumberland Street, Deansgate, MANCHESTER: 38 Northumberland Street, NEWCASTLE-ON-TYNE.

£295

The tremendous and ever-growing popularity of the Austin Twelve, and the arrangements we have made for vastly increased production, have enabled us to reduce the prices of all models very substantially indeed, so that they now range in price from £295 to £425 at Works. If you have denied yourself the joys of Austin ownership on the score of price, that bar to full motoring contentment is now entirely removed. The "Clifton" Tourer at £295 is undoubtedly the finest value in the motoring world to-day. In initial cost it compares favourably with any; in serviceable quality it far surpasses most.

SOURCE 13 An advert for a radio set. The BBC was set up in 1922, when 125,000 radio licences were issued

1. Can you work out what each of the numbered items in Source 12 would be used for?
2. If you were rich and had the money to afford all the items in Sources 9–13, in which order would you buy them? List them in order.
3. If you were poor and lived in the council house in Source 8, earning £3 per week and paying a rent of ten shillings (50p) per week, which items do you think you could afford?
4. Were any of these inventions useful in any way during the War on the Western Front?
5. Most of these items were not available before the War. Why do you think they appeared for sale shortly after the War ended?

Getting back to normal

In 1918 the government said that one of its aims was to get the country 'back to normal' – which for most people meant getting back to how things were before the War.

Most restrictions imposed under DORA (see page 52) were ended. Food RATIONING, for example, was gradually phased out: meat rationing ended in November 1919, butter rationing early in 1920 and sugar rationing in November 1920.

But other things could not be normalised so easily.

Industry – back to normal?

As you saw on page 9, before the War there were many strikes and industrial disputes. When the War broke out these were shelved. At first it was considered unpatriotic to complain about working conditions. Employers no longer kept to some of the existing laws which had protected workers against long hours and poor conditions. Shift work, Sunday work, short meal times and longer working days all became normal. Many of the women working in factories did so under much tougher conditions than men had had to put up with before the War. The government had enormous powers. Strikes were made illegal and in some industries the government even fixed the wages.

In 1916, when CONSCRIPTION was introduced, employers gained even more power over their workers because they were able to influence whether or not a worker was conscripted. An employer could prevent a skilled worker being called up if he said the worker was important. Some workers were afraid that if they asked for higher wages they would be sent to the trenches.

The government could not have produced all the weapons and food it needed during the War without the hard work and co-operation of the unions and the workers. And for much of the War the nation was united in supporting the changes in industry. But gradually unrest began to spread among the workers.

By 1917 food prices were twice what they had been in 1914. Workers demanded higher wages – particularly the railwaymen and the miners. In 1917 strikes started. There was even some talk of contacting German and Russian and French workers and agreeing not to fight any more. In Britain this was seen as treason.

After the War it was soon clear that industrial unrest had returned. The miners, railwaymen, cotton spinners and even the London police went on strike in 1918. In 1919 the railwaymen went on strike again, while the armed forces formed a union to try to get increased pay, shorter hours of duty and decent pensions. They also wanted a promise from the government that they would not be used as strike breakers. This really worried the government.

The War was followed by a trade slump around the world. By 1921 two million people in Britain were unemployed and employers began to reduce wages. This was the start of trouble in the coal industry that eventually led to the General Strike in 1926.

Meanwhile, the Labour Party, representing the growing trade union movement, had more MPs than ever before and was becoming a political force to be reckoned with.

SOURCE 14 Striking miners. A photograph taken in 1921

1. Look back at page 9. Would you say that problems in industry after the War were more or less serious than the problems before the War?
2. Did the War make the position of the unions in Britain stronger or weaker?
   Give reasons for both your answers.

Attitudes – back to normal?

Some historians say that the War brought about changes in people's attitudes which made it almost impossible to turn the clock back. The War had caused great divisions between the generations. Young people were no longer so willing to follow the advice or ideas of the older generation. The War had made many young people independent, whether they were teenage soldiers thrown into the conflict in France or women who had volunteered to work on the land or in the nursing services. They did not intend to give up this independence as soon as the War was over.

Many leading writers and artists were angry with the way the 'old men' had run the War. They were angry with the way the newspapers had hidden the truth about the War from the ordinary people. Very soon hard-hitting books and poems about the War began to appear.

But there were many people who simply wanted to forget the sadness and tragedy of the war years – even those who had lost members of their family in the fighting, or who had been injured themselves. They also wanted to forget the shortages and the restrictions of the war years. They wanted to enjoy themselves.

SOURCE 17 A cartoon of a 'flapper', drawn in 1925. A 'flapper' was a young woman who wore short skirts, cut her hair short, wore lots of make-up, smoked cigarettes and drank cocktails. These things may seem normal now, but it appeared very daring at the time and would have been disapproved of by many older people

SOURCE 15 Written by a Wiltshire farmer, A.G. Street, about the years 1918–21

❝ . . . We all had money to burn. I find this hard to write. It is not a pleasant thing to set down on paper what a tawdry life one lived in those few years . . . But the majority of farmers took no thought for tomorrow, their only idea was to have a good time. Instead of living for one's farm, the only desire was to get away from it and pursue pleasure elsewhere. ❞

SOURCE 16 From an interview with a Suffolk farm labourer, explaining why young soldiers would not become farm labourers

❝ The war had changed the men who had been in the army. They were better educated . . . They had a different feeling when they came back. They were not going to do the same things or put up with as much as they did afore they went out. ❞

1. Compare Source 17 with Source 12 on page 7. How has the style of dress changed?
2. Do you think that Sources 15–17 show that life in Britain was 'back to normal'?

Activity

Work in groups.

Take three large pieces of card. The first should have the heading 'Change for the better', the second one should have the heading 'No change', and the third 'Change for the worse'.

Using the information on pages 61–65, fill in each card using words and pictures. Use the finished cards to make a class display.

Was the War a turning point for women?

WOMEN were affected by all the changes we have examined in the last six pages. However, there were some changes which were particularly important for women. We are going to investigate two main issues:

■ Did the War change women's jobs?
■ Did the War get women the vote?

The right to work

During the War women did jobs that they had not been allowed to do before it. Many of them had reliable well paid employment for the first time. They were paid equal wages to men when they were doing 'men's work'. The money they earned gave their families a higher standard of nutrition and health. It also gave the women greater freedom and more importance in society.

While the War went on the government encouraged them to work outside their homes by introducing measures that made it easier. For example, the government was worried about the way the birth rate was falling. This was partly because women were not keen to have children if there was no one to look after them while they were working. They were also worried about bringing up babies in war conditions and when food was short. In July 1917 a 'National Baby Week' was held to demand better child welfare services. The number of child welfare centres was increased during the War from 350 to 578.

> **SOURCE 1** Report from the government's medical officers, 1919
>
> 66 *Most women enjoyed the more interesting, active and hard jobs, and in many cases their health improved rather than deteriorated. Women have with success undertaken work involving the lifting of weights, heavy machine work, and even forge and foundry work. This shows that light work is not by any means the most suitable for women. The conditions under which women worked before the War, low wages, poor diet, long hours and lack of exercise in the open air, resulted in poor physical health which led everyone to place too low a value on women's strength and capacity.* 99

> 1. How do Sources 1 and 2 differ in their views of women's employment during the War?
> 2. Can you think of reasons to explain their different viewpoints?

> **SOURCE 2** From a speech by the Suffragette leader Sylvia Pankhurst after the War
>
> 66 *Sometimes women wrote to me, broken down in health by overwork, complaining of long walks over sodden tracks, ankle deep in mud, to newly erected factories; of night shifts spent without even the possibility of getting a drink; of workers obliged to take their meals amidst the dust and fumes of the workshop.* 99

> **3.** In your opinion were the changes in women's employment during the War good or bad ones? Explain your answer.

However, after the War, as we have already seen, unemployment was a real problem. One obvious way of solving the problem of unemployment among ex-soldiers was to lay off women factory workers. This is what many employers decided to do. By 1919 around 750,000 women who had factory jobs before Armistice Day had been dismissed. Employers expected that they would simply return to the traditional women's jobs they had done before the War – domestic service, laundry work and dressmaking. Newspapers ran articles such as the one in Source 3 to persuade women to return to their old jobs.

> **SOURCE 3** From the *Southampton Times*, 1919
>
> 66 *Women still have not brought themselves to realise that factory work, with the money paid for it during the War, will not be possible again. Women who left domestic service to enter the factory are now required to return to the pots and pans.* 99

Some women did leave their jobs willingly. Married women with children, whose husbands returned from the War, were generally quite happy to stop work. Some women were not so willing, yet they had no choice, as Source 4 explains.

SOURCE 4 From the *Morning Post*, April 1919

"It has been found necessary to restrict, and in some cases to stop, unemployment benefit to ex-munitions workers in Sheffield. Three hundred women who have refused to accept work in domestic service have been suspended from all benefit."

MUNITIONS workers had often earned nearly £2 per week and they were not willing to go back to earning less than £1.

Source 6 shows what happened to a group of nine women in Southampton. Of these nine only Mrs Brady said she was happy to return to her pre-war job, although Mrs Gregory thought it was only fair to make way for a man.

Some women did keep their jobs, particularly those working in offices and shops, but this sort of work was becoming less popular with men in any case. It seemed that in many ways attitudes to women's work had not been changed by the War. By 1921 the proportion of women who had a job was smaller than it had been before the War, and women's unemployment was a major problem.

SOURCE 5 This young Southampton girl drove a bread delivery van throughout the War, but had to give up when the men came home. She said, 'I cried when I had to come off the [bread] round. I didn't think it was fair; but of course, men were coming home from the War and men wanted jobs. So to see a girl driving round with a pony and cart was not in it'

SOURCE 6 Work done by women in Southampton during and after the War

	War work	After the war
Mrs Stone	farm worker	domestic service
Mrs Bell	Pirelli factory	domestic service
Mrs Gregory	engineer at Avro	domestic service
Mrs Mullins	government mill	nurse on a liner, then left to get married
Mrs Brady	munitions factory	dressmaking
Mrs Kilford	office work	office work
Mrs Barnet	telegraph operator	housewife, looking after child
Mrs Hayes	transport worker	cleaner
Mrs Ottaway	van driver	van driver, but left to get married

SOURCE 7 From the *Liverpool Daily Post*, January 1919

"One would think, to hear some people talk, that the whole problem of women's unemployment is to be solved in the near future by a general 'back to the kitchen' movement on the part of ex-munitions workers. Certainly the ordinary man in the street holds that view, but it is not the true one. It is simply a continuation of the old idea that a woman's place is in the home, and if she does not happen to have one of her own, she had best make herself useful in someone else's."

4. Of the newspaper reports in Sources 3, 4 and 7, which take the side of women who wish to work?
5. What reasons might the women in Sources 4, 5 or 6 give for not wishing to return to domestic service or other 'women's' jobs?
6. Why do you think the women in Source 6 who married gave up work?

The attitude of many women had changed as a result of the War. Their unwillingness to go into domestic service was seen as a big enough problem for it to be raised in Cabinet. The Cabinet set up a committee to look into the problem. Source 8 gives extracts from its report.

SOURCE 8 A report presented to Parliament in 1919

There is among girls a growing distaste for domestic service under its present conditions and a reluctance on the part of parents to allow them to take up such work . . .

Domestic workers are regarded by other workers as belonging to a lower social status . . . The hours compare unfavourably with any other occupation . . .

As a result the occupation is mainly carried on by unskilled workers who are unable on the one hand to command for themselves satisfactory conditions of employment, or on the other to fulfil their tasks efficiently.

We regard the position as serious in that the best use is not being made of an occupation which might under other conditions . . . be attractive to, and most suitable for, a large section of women workers of the nation.

The committee recommended some important changes to make domestic service a more attractive occupation for working-class women: reduced hours, fixed mealtimes, days off, paid holidays, changed uniform, better food and the introduction of mechanical appliances to help servants do boring and time-consuming jobs. But their report was shelved by the government and no action was taken. It was left for working women either to vote with their feet and leave domestic service, even though many other jobs were closed to them, or to tolerate the low status and poor conditions in order to have some money coming in. You can see from Source 9 how the number of women working in domestic service after the War changed.

However, the government did take more action about job opportunities for educated women. In 1919 it passed the Sex Disqualification Removal Act. This opened up a number of professions to women for the first time. Women could now become barristers, solicitors, auctioneers, surveyors, architects or judges, and could serve on a jury.

1. Compare Source 9 with Source 1 on page 8. Has women's employment returned to normal?
2. Look at Source 10. What does it tell you about what a woman's role in the 1920s was seen to be?

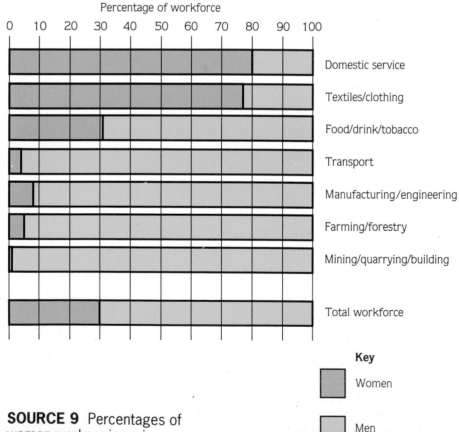

Percentage of workforce

Domestic service

Textiles/clothing

Food/drink/tobacco

Transport

Manufacturing/engineering

Farming/forestry

Mining/quarrying/building

Total workforce

Key

Women

Men

SOURCE 9 Percentages of women workers in various industries in 1931

SOURCE 10 The front cover of the magazine *Woman's World*, 25 June 1927, showing a housewife's weekly work

The right to vote

Before the War, leaders of the SUFFRAGETTE movement had campaigned quite violently to get women the vote (see pages 10–11). Once the War began, they stopped direct action and threw their energy into the war effort.

During the War there was no General Election. But in 1916 the government decided to set up a committee to plan for the election that would be called as soon as the War was over. The government was worried that under current voting laws most soldiers would not be able to vote, because they had been away from their homes for more than twelve months. The committee was meant to reform voting laws so that members of the armed forces could vote. However, women seized this opportunity to press their demands to be given the vote.

SOURCE 11 Written by Mrs Pankhurst in the magazine *Women's Dreadnought* on 3 June 1916

The forthcoming Bill is supposed to extend the vote to additional numbers of men . . . The Tory press says it will 'give votes to our soldiers and sailors' . . .

Demonstrations and conferences must be held, petitions organised from every district. The demand must be sent to Parliament that there shall be no half measures . . . but a Franchise Bill to give the vote to every woman and man over 21 . . .

The next few weeks are of vital importance. We must use them in working for Human Suffrage with all the energy we possess.

VOTES FOR HEROINES AS WELL AS HEROES

CHIVALRY: "Men and women protect one another in the hour of death. With the addition of the woman's vote, they would be able to protect one another in life as well."

SOURCE 12 A cartoon from the cover of *Votes for Women* magazine, 26 November 1915

Activity

It is 1925. You have been called to give evidence to a committee looking into employment opportunities for women.

What evidence will you give the committee that:
a) the War raised women's expectations of a good job
b) the post-war period has not fulfilled their expectations?

You may wish to refer to pages 54–55.

The conference opened on 12 October 1916. One of the Suffragette leaders, Millicent Fawcett, negotiated with Cabinet officials and an agreement was reached. Women would be given the vote, but – so that women voters would not outnumber men voters – the vote would not be given to *all* women. When the committee made its report it suggested that married women over 30 should be allowed to vote.

David Lloyd George was the new Prime Minister. Before the war his Liberal Party had been split on what to do about women's SUFFRAGE. But it was Lloyd George who had asked for Mrs Pankhurst's help in 1915 to get women to work in the munitions factories. He recognised the role women had played in the war effort. In 1917 he put through Parliament a Bill to give women the vote. And so, in December 1917, Parliament gave the vote to six million of Britain's eleven million adult women. There were only 23 votes against. The Bill became law in 1918.

> **SOURCE 13** A speech made by Lloyd George in 1918
>
> 66 It would have been utterly impossible for us to have won the War had it not been for the skill, enthusiasm and industry which the women of this country have thrown into the War. 99

Many MPs had changed their minds. Before the War, one of the most determined opponents of women's suffrage had been Herbert Asquith, who was Prime Minister until 1916. But by 1917 he had made a public U-turn (see Source 14).

> **SOURCE 14** A speech made by Asquith in Parliament in 1917
>
> 66 How could we have carried on the War without women? . . . Wherever we turn we see them doing work which three years ago we would have regarded as being exclusively 'men's work'. But what I confess moves me still more in this matter is the problem of what to do when the War is over. The questions will then arise about women's labour and women's functions in the new order of things. I would find it impossible to withhold from women the power and the right of making their voices directly heard. 99

1. Look at Source 14. Why does Asquith say he has changed his mind about women voting?
2. Why do you think Mrs Pankhurst would be
   a) pleased, and b) displeased with the new law in 1918? Explain your answer.

Why 1918?

Why did women get the vote in 1918? Was it because the actions of women like the Suffragettes forced the government to give them the right to vote? Or was it because women had shown by the part that they played during the War that they should have the same rights as men?

Below are some of the arguments put forward by historians about why women got the vote in 1918.

1. What do you think? How did each of the following factors help women get the vote in 1918:
   ■ the actions of the Suffragettes
   ■ women's war effort?

The war effort gave ordinary women more confidence in their abilities, and so more confidence in pressing for the vote by political argument.

Suffrage had been extending gradually anyway for the last 100 years. The inclusion of women was bound to come some time. The Suffragette activity and the women's war effort were simply the triggers that helped it to happen in 1918.

1918 and afterwards

The first women candidates stood for Parliament in the 1918 election, and in 1919 women were sitting as MPs in Parliament for the first time. In 1928, all adult women were granted the vote on the same terms as men. Laws were passed that began to improve the situation of women in various areas of their lives. We have already seen how the professions were opened up to women in 1919. In 1923 women gained equal rights to men in divorce proceedings. In 1925 the Civil Service admitted women. In 1930 the Ministry of Health began to make advice on contraception available to women.

1. Write a short essay with the title: 'Was the War a turning point for women?'. Use the information on pages 66–71.
   You will need to consider:
   ■ what the situation of women – both poor and rich – was before the War
   ■ how their situation changed during the War
   ■ how their situation changed after the War.
   Then draw some conclusions about whether the War was a turning point.

You have now studied what Britain was like before the War, during the War and after the War. You are going to create a wall display called 'Changing Britain'.

1. Look back at pages 4–11. Use words and pictures to show how Britain after the War was different from Britain before it.
2. Working in groups, decide which of these changes a) would have happened even without the war, b) happened because of the War.
3. On your own, write three paragraphs to explain whether you think the War made Britain a better place to live.

> Without the violent campaign the Suffragettes fought before the War, no one would ever have taken their cause seriously and the government would have kept on postponing a decision, thinking that it was not an important issue. The Suffragette campaign was proof that women wanted the vote, and wanted it enough to go to prison for it.

> The violence of the Suffragettes actually held back women's suffrage because it lost them the popular support they had. They could have had the vote much earlier than 1918. Their violent campaigns made the government more determined not to give in.

> Prior to the War many men did not see women as capable. But the women's war effort changed forever the way many men saw women and they could no longer support an electoral system that excluded them from voting.

Glossary

airship a large balloon filled with hydrogen or helium gas, with a cabin for people to travel in and steer. Could carry bombs and a machine gunner. The first airships were invented by a German, Count von Zeppelin, in 1900, and German airships were known as Zeppelins after him

Allies the countries fighting against Germany in the Great War: Britain, France, Russia (until 1917), the USA (from 1917) and several others

armistice a truce, when both sides agree to stop fighting for a time

artillery heavy guns. The Royal Artillery is the part of the army which uses them

atrocities particularly cruel, violent acts against other people, usually when they are defenceless

battery a group of heavy guns (**artillery**)

bayonet a stabbing blade that can be attached to the end of a rifle

billet the illegal buying and selling of **rationed** goods

bombardment non-stop firing of heavy guns

cavalry soldiers on horseback

censor to look at letters, films, newspapers, etc. and remove parts that might give useful information to the enemy

civilian a person who is not in the armed services

coalition a temporary alliance of political parties to form a government

commandeer to take over or seize for military use

conscription a law that forced all men between eighteen and 41 to join the armed forces if they were needed

court martial a military court. To court martial someone is to try them in a military court

dressing station a place for giving emergency treatment to the wounded

drill strict training for parades: how to stand, march, hold weapons etc.

dugout a roofed shelter built into the wall of a trench

front line the land nearest the enemy, where the fighting takes place

infantry foot-soldiers, the main part of the army

leave a period of time when a soldier is allowed to leave the battle and go home

munitions weapons, amunition, equipment, etc.

neutral a country that is not part of any alliances and does not fight in wars

pacifist somebody who is opposed to any sort of war, or to violence for any reason

patriotism love of one's country and willingness to defend it against attack

propaganda limited, often biased, information which is spread about to persuade people to support certain ideas or government policies

ration, rationing to give each person a fixed official amount of certain sorts of food or other goods, e.g. coal, when they are in short supply

reconnaissance a survey of an area to find important features, or the enemy's position

shell an explosive missile or bomb fired from a heavy gun

stalemate a situation in a battle when neither army can gain any ground

suffrage the right to vote in political elections

Suffragette a woman who tried to get the vote by means of sometimes violent protests

Western Front the area of Northern France and Belgium in which battles were fought. Fighting also took place in Russia, Italy and Turkey